Roderick J. Watts
Robert J. Jagers
Editors

Manhood Development
in Urban
African-American Communities

Manhood Development in Urban African-American Communities has been co-published simultaneously as *Journal of Prevention & Intervention in the Community*, Volume 16, Numbers 1/2 1997.

Pre-publication
REVIEWS,
COMMENTARIES,
EVALUATIONS . . .

"**W**atts and Jagers provide the much needed foundational and baseline information and research that begins to philosophically and empirically validate the importance of understanding culture, oppression, and gender when working with males in urban African-American communities."

Paul Hill, Jr., MSW, LISW, ACSW
East End Neighborhood House
Cleveland, Ohio

Manhood Development in Urban African-American Communities

Manhood Development in Urban African-American Communities has been co-published simultaneously as *Journal of Prevention & Intervention in the Community*, Volume 16, Numbers 1/2 1997.

Manhood Development in Urban African-American Communities

Roderick J. Watts
Robert J. Jagers
Editors

Manhood Development in Urban African-American Communities has been co-published simultaneously as *Journal of Prevention & Intervention in the Community,* Volume 16, Numbers 1/2, 1997.

The Haworth Press, Inc.
New York • London

Manhood Development in Urban African-American Communities has been co-published simultaneously as *Journal of Prevention & Intervention in the Community*, Volume 16, Numbers 1/2 1997.

The development, preparation, and publication of this work has been undertaken with great care. However, the publisher, employees, editors, and agents of The Haworth Press and all imprints of The Haworth Press, Inc., including The Haworth Medical Press and Pharmaceutical Products Press, are not responsible for any errors contained herein or for consequences that may ensue from use of materials or information contained in this work. Opinions expressed by the author(s) are not necessarily those of The Haworth Press, Inc.

Cover design by Thomas J. Mayshock Jr.

The Haworth Press, Inc., 10 Alice Street, Binghamton, NY 13904-1580 USA

Library of Congress Cataloging-in-Publication Data

Manhood development in urban African-American communities / Roderick J. Watts, Robert J. Jagers, editors.
     p. cm.
    "Co-published simultaneously as Journal of prevention & intervention in the community, volume 16, numbers 1/2, 1997."
    Includes bibliographical references and index.
    ISBN 0-7890-0377-5 (alk. paper).–ISBN 0-7890-0505-0 (pbk.:alk.paper)
    1. Afro-American men–Psychology. 2. Afro-American men–Social conditions. 3. Masculinity–United States. I. Watts, Roderick J. II. Jagers, Robert J.
E185.86.M362 1997   97-45551
305.38′896073–dc21   CIP

INDEXING & ABSTRACTING

Contributions to this publication are selectively indexed or abstracted in print, electronic, online, or CD-ROM version(s) of the reference tools and information services listed below. This list is current as of the copyright date of this publication. See the end of this section for additional notes.

- *Abstracts of Research in Pastoral Care & Counseling*, Loyola College, 7135 Minstrel Way, Suite 101, Columbia, MD 21045
- *Behavioral Medicine Abstracts,* University of Washington, Department of Social Work & Speech & Hearing Sciences, Box 354900, Seattle, WA 98195
- *Child Development Abstracts & Bibliography*, University of Kansas, 213 Bailey Hall, Lawrence, KS 66045
- *CNPIEC Reference Guide: Chinese National Directory of Foreign Periodicals*, P.O. Box 88, Beijing, Peoples Republic of China
- *Excerpta Medica/Secondary Publishing Division*, Elsevier Science Inc., Secondary Publishing Division, 655 Avenue of the Americas, New York, NY 10010
- *Family Studies Database (online and CD/ROM),* National Information Services Corporation, 306 East Baltimore Pike, 2nd Floor, Media, PA 19063
- *HealthPromis*, Health Education Authority (HEA)/Health Promotion Information Centre, Hamilton House-Mabledon Place, London WC1H 9TX, England
- *IBZ International Bibliography of Periodical Literature,* Zeller Verlag GmbH & Co., P.O.B. 1949, d-49009 Osnabruck, Germany
- *INTERNET ACCESS (& additional networks) Bulletin Board for Libraries ("BUBL"), coverage of information resources on INTERNET, JANET, and other networks.*
  - <URL:http://bubl.ac.uk/>
  - The new locations will be found under <URL:http://bubl.ac. uk/link/>.
  - Any existing BUBL users who have problems finding information on the new service should contact the BUBL help line by sending e-mail to <bubl@bubl.ac.uk>.
  The Andersonian Library, Curran Building, 101 St. James Road, Glasgow G4 0NS, Scotland
- *Mental Health Abstracts (online through DIALOG)*, IFI/Plenum Data Company, 3202 Kirkwood Highway, Wilmington, DE 19808
- *National Clearinghouse on Child Abuse & Neglect,* 10530 Rosehaven Street, Suite 400, Fairfax, VA 22030-2804
- *NIAAA Alcohol and Alcohol Problems Science Database (ETOH),* National Institute on Alcohol Abuse and Alcoholism, 1400 Eye Street NW, Suite 600, Washington, DC 20005
- *OT BibSys,* American Occupational Therapy Foundation, P.O. Box 31220, Rockville, MD 20824-1220

(continued)

- *Referativnyi Zhurnal (Abstracts Journal of the Institute of Scientific Information of the Republic of Russia)*, The Institute of Scientific Information, Baltijskaja ul., 14, Moscow A-219, Republic of Russia

- *RMDB DATABASE (Reliance Medical Information)*, Reliance Medical Information, Inc. (RMI), 100 Putnam Green, Greenwich, CT 06830

- *Social Planning/Policy & Development Abstracts (SOPODA)*, Sociological Abstracts, Inc., P. O. Box 22206, San Diego, CA 92192-0206

- *Social Work Abstracts*, National Association of Social Workers, 750 First Street NW, 8th Floor, Washington, DC 20002

- *Sociological Abstracts (SA)*, Sociological Abstracts, Inc., P. O. Box 22206, San Diego, CA 92192-0206

- *SOMED (social medicine) Database*, Landes Institut fur Den Offentlichen Gesundheitsdienst NRW, Postfach 20 10 12, D-33548 Bielefeld, Germany

- *Violence and Abuse Abstracts: A Review of Current Literature on Interpersonal Violence (VAA)*, Sage Publications, Inc., 2455 Teller Road, Newbury Park, CA 91320

SPECIAL BIBLIOGRAPHIC NOTES

related to special journal issues (separates) and indexing/abstracting

❏ indexing/abstracting services in this list will also cover material in any "separate" that is co-published simultaneously with Haworth's special thematic journal issue or DocuSerial. Indexing/abstracting usually covers material at the article/chapter level.

❏ monographic co-editions are intended for either non-subscribers or libraries which intend to purchase a second copy for their circulating collections.

❏ monographic co-editions are reported to all jobbers/wholesalers/approval plans. The source journal is listed as the "series" to assist the prevention of duplicate purchasing in the same manner utilized for books-in-series.

❏ to facilitate user/access services all indexing/abstracting services are encouraged to utilize the co-indexing entry note indicated at the bottom of the first page of each article/chapter/contribution.

❏ this is intended to assist a library user of any reference tool (whether print, electronic, online, or CD-ROM) to locate the monographic version if the library has purchased this version but not a subscription to the source journal.

❏ individual articles/chapters in any Haworth publication are also available through the Haworth Document Delivery Service (HDDS).

Manhood Development in Urban African-American Communities

CONTENTS

ABOUT THE EDITORS

Roderick J. Watts, PhD, is a community psychologist and clinical psychologist currently working as Associate Professor of Psychology and Director of Clinical Psychology Training at DePaul University in Chicago, Illinois. His action and research interests include manhood development, human diversity, oppression theory, sociopolitical development, racial identity, and qualitative research methodology. He has served as a program development and evaluation consultant on manhood development and diversity to governmental organizations, schools, foundations, research and public policy organizations, universities, and other nonprofit organizations. The co-editor of the book *Human Diversity, Perspectives on People in Context*, Dr. Watts has held positions at The Consultation Center at Yale University and the Institute for Urban Affairs and Research at Howard University.

Robert J. Jagers, PhD, is Associate Professor of African-American Studies and Psychology and Interim Head of the Department of African-American Studies at the University of Illinois at Chicago. He is Co-Principal Investigator (PI) on a National Institute of Child Health and Human Development (NICHD) research grant, "The Chicago African-American Youth Health Behaviors Project." He is also the PI on the community-based "Fisher of Men Project" funded by the Amoco Foundation. Both projects are concerned with the development, implementation, and evaluation of culturally appropriate interventions for inner-city African-American youth. Dr. Jagers is a core faculty member, supervising one pre-doctoral and one post-doctoral student, on a National Institutes of Mental Health research and training grant on urban children's mental health and HIV/AIDS prevention.

Dr. Jagers recently received the Eighth Annual APA Minority Fellowship Achievement Award for Research. His research interests are in African-American culture and social development of children and youth. He is especially concerned with understanding the multiple cultural experiences and resultant orientations of urban youth and the ways in which these factors influence their pro-social development.

Manhood Development:
Concepts and Strategies

Roderick J. Watts

DePaul University

Robert J. Jagers

University of Illinois at Chicago

THEMES IN MANHOOD DEVELOPMENT

No matter where or how they are portrayed and examined, African-American men are the object of much attention. In the popular press, in academic circles, on the television screen–wherever–there is much discussion and debate. Drugs, teenage pregnancy, gang warfare, crime (from O.J. Simpson to Mumia Abu Jamal), and fiery leadership (Louis Farrakhan) are frequently associated in the public mind with African-American men. Although sometimes called "an endangered species" (Gibbs, 1988) Black men loom large on the urban landscape.

This volume on African-American men begins with the assumption that culture, oppression, and gender are the major themes we must understand to promote the positive development of young, African-American men. However, the salience and character of these themes varies depending on context. This volume focuses on

---

[Haworth co-indexing entry note]: "Manhood Development: Concepts and Strategies." Watts, Roderick J., and Robert J. Jagers. Co-published simultaneously in *Journal of Prevention & Intervention in the Community* (The Haworth Press, Inc.) Vol. 16, No. 1/2, 1997, pp. 1-5; and: *Manhood Development in Urban African-American Communities* (ed: Roderick J. Watts, and Robert J. Jagers) The Haworth Press, Inc., 1997, pp. 1-5. Single or multiple copies of this article are available for a fee from The Haworth Document Delivery Service [1-800-342-9678, 9:00 a.m. - 5:00 p.m. (EST). E-mail address: getinfo@haworth.com].

1

urban ecologies because they have the largest concentration of Black men, and it is where most of the contributors have done their work. We recognize that the work in this volume takes a particular focus. The contributors do not directly address, for example, the specific circumstances of rural, suburban, gay or affluent men. We hope these aspects of within-group diversity get addressed as the area of manhood development expands and evolves. In this introduction, we will briefly discuss three recurring themes among the contributors–culture, oppression and gender.

THE CENTRALITY OF CULTURE AND ENCULTURATION

African-Americans are more than a racial group. As well as being defined by this socially-constructed category African-Americans have an ethnicity based on West African culture that has been evolving in the US for nearly 400 years. Interdisciplinary work in Black studies and more recently Afrocentrism (Asante, 1989) are part of a scholarly effort to understand the cultural as well as sociopolitical components of the Black experience. Culture is central because implicitly or explicitly, it is the backdrop for all human thought and action. Although there are a multitude of definitions of culture–back in 1952, Kroeber and Kluckhohn found 164, none of which was adopted by everyone either up to that time or since (Lonner, 1994). The definition Kroeber and Kluckhohn arrived at ten years after their analysis is, nonetheless, a useful one:

> Culture consists of patterns, explicit and implicit, of and for behavior acquired and transmitted by symbols, constituting the distinctive achievement of human groups, including their embodiments of artifacts; the essential core of culture consists of traditional (i.e., historically derived and selected) ideas and especially their attached values; cultural systems may, on one hand, be considered products of actions, on the other hand, as conditioning elements of further action. (cited in Veroff & Goldberger, 1995, p. 357)

Culture provides a basic template for guiding humans around the world as they address common concerns of education, gender and elder roles, sexuality, and so on. For members of ethnic groups, the process of enculturation (that is, the initial transmission of culture to the young) is especially challenging, because by definition ethnic groups co-exist as part of a larger cultural system. Less powerful groups face competition from those that dominate. As an ethnic group with a history of enslavement, African-Americans occupy a uniquely challenging position in the Americas. The most overt, recognizable aspects of their culture were deliberately obliterated and undermined as part of the so-called seasoning process that transformed continental Africans into enslaved US Africans. Nonetheless, "Africanisms" persisted, and continue today as part of African-American ethnicity (Jones, 1991). But the issue of culture and identity is complex. The age-old question articulated by Du-Bois (1961) of double-consciousness (African or American?) continues to spark much debate about the optimal enculturation for people of African descent in the US.

Many theorists, researchers and activists are working to rediscover, reconstruct, and reanimate the African worldview as a means of uplifting the African diaspora. Jagers's article (this volume) is an example of the basic, empirical research that can help establish a philosophical, theoretical and empirical foundation for African-American enculturation. Ghee, Walker, and Younger's (this volume) "Edutainment" approach to cultural socialization illustrates how philosophical and cultural ideas can make the transition from abstractions to engaging activities in manhood development. The article by Warfield-Coppock (this volume) examines gender in an African cultural context and highlights traditional rites of passage training. She links manhood and womanhood development in a single, holistic model. Just as women's studies and men's studies are being linked through gender studies, the development of men and women can benefit from an integrated, culturally-conscious model. How else can we properly prepare the two genders for working together?

OPPRESSION AND LIBERATION

In the U.S. and elsewhere, African physical features are a social marker for oppression as well as for ethnicity. It is a social and political construction with adverse consequences for African people regardless of their ethnic identity. The battle for liberation from oppression continues, and Africans in the Americas have a very long history of political and spiritual culture in support of social change. It is a culture where the material and spiritual worlds are seen as complementary rather than antagonistic. Warfield-Coppock and Mattis (both in this volume) highlight spirituality's role.

Along with the material and spiritual dimensions of liberation activity, there are the personal and collective dimensions. Stevenson's article (this volume) on racial socialization explores how African-Americans *personally* cope with and combat oppression and struggle to develop a healthy ethnic identity. As a complement, Watts and Abdul-Adil's article describes theory and action that fosters a systemic view of oppression, and ultimately an impulse to act *collectively*.

GENDER

Racial oppression and White supremacy are worldwide phenomena but so is the gender-based oppression of women (Ani, 1994; Brittan & Maynard, 1984). Gender roles in African-American communities typically reproduce the sexism of the dominant culture (Collins, 1991). Africentrists such as Ani have argued that prevailing notions of masculinity (e.g., the ruthless and competitive pursuit of power, control, material wealth, and social status) are part of the legacy of European cultures, and many, including Warfield-Coppock (this volume), describe a less hierarchical and more complementary conception of gender in traditional African societies. Regardless of the origin of contemporary U.S. masculinity, encouraging African-American men to emulate White men and others in these negative ways is unlikely to be successful, and failures can undermine self esteem and increase stress. More importantly, it would widen and strengthen sexism. Therefore, a critical perspective on gender with an eye to a more socially-beneficial construction of it is fundamental to manhood development. Warfield-Coppock's article helps us understand how principles from African cosmology and culture can aid in a culturally-conscious reconstruction of gender.

REFERENCES

Ani, M. (1994). *Yurugu: An African-centered critique of European cultural thought and behavior.* Trenton, NJ: African World Press.

Asante, M.K. (1988). *Afrocentricity.* Trenton: African World Press.

Brittan, A., & Maynard, M. (1984). *Sexism, Racism, and Oppression.* New York: Basil Blackwell Publisher Ltd.

Bulhan, H. (1988). *Franz Fanon and the psychology of oppression.* New York: Plenum. p. vii.

Collins, P. (1991). *Black Feminist Thought.* Chapter 1. The politics of Black feminist thought (pp. 1-18). NY: Routledge.

DuBois, W.E. (1961). *The souls of Black folk.* New York: Fawcett.

Gibbs, J.T. (1988). *Young, Black, and male in America; An endangered species.* Dover, MA: Auburn House Publishing Company.

Jones, J. (1991). Psychological models of race: What have they been and what should they be? In J. Goodchilds (ed.), *Psychological perspectives on human diversity in America.* Washington DC: American Psychological Association.

Lonner, W (1994). Culture and human diversity. In E. Trickett, R. Watts, & D. Birman (eds.), *Human Diversity: perspectives on people in context.* San Francisco: Jossey-Bass.

Veroff & Goldberger (1995). *The Culture and Psychology Reader.* NY: New York University Press.

Afrocultural Integrity and the Social Development of African-American Children: Some Conceptual, Empirical, and Practical Considerations

Robert J. Jagers

University of Illinois at Chicago

SUMMARY. In this paper the role of culture in the social development of African-American youth was explored, and an Afrocultural social ethos was advanced as a concept for investigating the social functioning. Study 1 found no significant gender differences on the social ethos variable in third and sixth graders (47 boys, 43 girls) ratings of self, family or friends. However, boys reported more delinquent behaviors than did girls, and friend's social ethos was predictive of fewer aggressive and delinquent behaviors. Although no significant gender differences on social ethos emerged among the sixth and seventh graders (54 boys, 47 girls) in Study 2, family ethos was predictive of empathic concern while the ethos of friends predicted greater perspective taking. Gender was the only significant predictor of peer-rated helping behavior, with girls judged to demonstrate such behaviors more than boys. Discussion focused on directions for basic and applied research, with an emphasis on African-American men and the importance of mobilizing indigenous community resources. *[Article copies available for a fee from The Haworth Document Delivery Service: 1-800-342-9678. E-mail address: getinfo@haworth.com]*

[Haworth co-indexing entry note]: "Afrocultural Integrity and the Social Development of African-American Children: Some Conceptual, Empirical, and Practical Considerations." Jagers, Robert J. Co-published simultaneously in *Journal of Prevention & Intervention in the Community* (The Haworth Press, Inc.) Vol. 16, No. 1/2, 1997, pp. 7-34; and: *Manhood Development in Urban African-American Communities* (ed: Roderick J. Watts, and Robert J. Jagers) The Haworth Press, Inc., 1997, pp. 7-34. Single or multiple copies of this article are available for a fee from The Haworth Document Delivery Service [1-800-342-9678, 9:00 a.m. - 5:00 p.m. (EST). E-mail address: getinfo@haworth.com].

7

Over the past decade culture has reemerged as a potentially useful lens through which social scientists might view the life experiences of both foreign and domestic cultural groups (e.g., Berry, Poortinga, Segall & Dasen, 1992; Betancourt & Lopez, 1993; Greenfield & Cocking, 1994; Shweder, 1991). This trend, together with the assertion of an Africentric perspective, has sparked greater acknowledgment that the present day African-American experience features both African and European American cultural realms (Boykin, 1983; Jones, 1991). However, there remains much to be done in terms of fleshing out the nature and relevance of African (or what will be referred to as Afrocultural) phenomena among extant African-Americans. Not only have certain Afrocultural motifs been romanticized (Dei, 1994), but conceptual fuzziness and a dearth of basic empirical research have resulted in virtually no documentation of the degree to which Afrocultural values, beliefs and behaviors are embraced within an increasingly diverse African-American community. By extension, the literature is largely silent on the psychological implications of such motifs. Attempting to fill this sizable void is of considerable importance. For, even if African-Americans were shown to have retained aspects of their African past, the absence of valued psychological ramifications would raise serious questions about the utility of such carryovers.

Systematic examination of these matters becomes basic to discussions of what constitutes a healthy, well-functioning African-American adult. Such scholarship would seem to be pivotal to an integrity-based formulation of desirable developmental goals, benchmarks and pathways for African-American youth. Still further, the urgent need to enhance the life chances of youth, particularly those from poor inner-city communities, makes these endeavors invaluable to culturally appropriate preventive and secondary interventions.

This paper seeks to contribute to scholarship in this area. After a cursory treatment of concepts pertinent to the study of culture, the notion of Afrocultural integrity was discussed. The notion of an Afrocultural social ethos is defined and advanced as an integrity based construct for investigating the social functioning of African-American youth. A brief review of the social development of African children and youth revealed an emphasis placed on good character and to the role of family, peers and the broader community in its cultivation. This analysis was then extended to the African-American experience. Family and friends were viewed as the primary contexts in which Afrocultural learning occurs, and character is promoted. A few examples of conceptions of character were drawn from available psychological literature in this connection.

Two preliminary studies into these matters were presented. Study 1 examined developmental and gender trends on an Afrocultural social ethos among third and sixth grade boys and girls. Gender, youth's ethos and their perceptions of their family and friend's ethos were used as predictors of aggressive, delinquent and social withdrawal behaviors. Study 2 examined gender differences on the Afrocultural social ethos variables between sixth and seventh grade inner-city boys and girls. It also attempted to predict empathic concern, perspective taking and peer nominated helping behaviors using gender, youth's ethos, and their perceptions of the ethos of family and friends.

Finally, some directions for basic and applied research, with an emphasis on African-American men were discussed. In terms of a research agenda, the need for inquiry into issues of morality was emphasized. The discussion of interventions placed a focus on the prospects and impediments for marshaling indigenous community resources to support of the development of healthy, well-functioning African-American boys and men.

CULTURE

Culture helps to frame notions of optimal human development and its associated benchmarks and pathways (Greenfield, 1994). Although culture has historically been outside the purview of psychologists, the movement toward more contextualized understanding of variations in human psychological functioning have made cultural analyses more appealing. The concept has been made more available to the psychological enterprise through the delineation of its various aspects. For instance, it has been suggested that culture comprises subjective and objective elements (Triandis, 1972), deep and surface structures (Myers, 1991) and symbolic and material components (Greenfield, 1994). Generally speaking, these distinctions indicate that culture is both within its participants (intrapsychic), and is also reflected in the surrounding milieu. Boykin (1993) has offered a more fine-grained analysis, suggesting that a given culture has functional, expressive, structural and fundamental elements. Briefly, functional culture includes concrete skills, practices and indigenous psychologies. Expressive culture refers to symbolic systems (e.g., language, numbers), customs, creative artifacts and recreational activities. Laws or codes, communication forms and institutions are captured under structural culture. Finally, fundamental culture connotes world views, sensibilities and behavioral inclinations.

It is assumed that fundamental culture provides a set of presuppositions which influence functional, expressive, and/or structural manifestations. This position is not inconsistent with Shweder (1991) who defines culture as an intentional or constituted world whose existence and meaning are predicated upon human involvement and interpretation. The term cultural orientation is employed in our work to represent individual differences in resonance with a particular fundamental cultural theme. Both self-identification and preference are incorporated into this notion. Self-identification connotes the degree to which one believes that they possess or demonstrate qualities associated with a specified cultural dimension. Preference refers to the appeal or desirability of a cultural theme. Our nascent work has focused on the functional significance of cultural orientations, attempting to discern what correspondence, if any, they have with psychological processes and outcomes.

It seems likely that structural aspects of cultures help to provide a normative framework for individual and collective development. These structures help to transmit and to refine prescribed cultural patterning across the life span. We have an interest in the degree to which various cultural agents (e.g., family, peers, church, school and media), act to promote or to discourage specific cultural motifs. We assume that cultural learning occurs largely through enculturation (Herskovits, 1955). Enculturation refers to the process by which persons acquire contents and perspectives of their cultural milieu without explicit instruction or training (Berry et al., 1992). For us, this has translated into a focus on the degree to which youth's perceptions of the cultural orientations of their family and friends influence their own cultural dispositions, and their related psychological processes and outcomes.

AFROCULTURAL INTEGRITY

Contemporary work on the Afrocultural integrity of African-Americans was stimulated by the Black liberation movements of the 1960s. During this era, African-American scholars began to question the presuppositions which undergirded their and others' understanding of African-American life (e.g., Boykin, 1983; Nobles,1991). Cultural variant and cultural difference approaches were advanced as challenges to prevailing notions of cultural deficiency and pathology. Ostensibly, it was argued that although African-Americans increasingly participated in mainstream American society, they did not necessarily subscribe to its underlying Anglo-cultural tenets. Not only had a history of White racism and oppression produced an array of reactionary stances and strategies, but African-Americans also had their own unique set of cultural imperatives which evolve out of their African heritage (e.g., Jones, 1991).

A substantial body of historical and anthropological literature detailing the persistence of African cultural themes among African ancestried people was available to interested psychologists (e.g., DuBois, 1939; Franklin & Moss, 1988; Herskovits, 1958; Holloway, 1990; Thompson, 1983; Stuckey, 1987; Woodson, 1968). Among those psychologists concerned with African retentions (e.g., Baldwin, 1991; Boykin, 1983; Jones, 1991; Nobles, 1991), the work of Boykin and colleagues deserves particular attention (e.g., Boykin, 1983; Boykin & Toms, 1985; Boykin & Ellison, 1995). In the context of their broader conceptual framework, they submit that the Afrocultural realm of the African-American experience is comprised of at least nine interrelated dimensions. These dimensions and a summary definition are provided below:

- *spirituality*–connotes an acknowledgment of a nonmaterial force that permeates all affairs, human and nonhuman
- *affect*–implies the centrality of affective information and emotional expressiveness linked to the co-importance of feelings and thoughts

- *communalism*–denotes a paramount commitment to the fundamental interdependence of people and to social bonds and relationships
- *orality*–connotes the centrality of oral/aural modes of communication for conveying true meaning and to cultivating speaking as a performance
- *verve*–implies an especial receptiveness to relatively high levels of sensate stimulation
- *social time perspective*–denotes a commitment to time as a social construction such that there is an event orientation toward time
- *harmony*–implies that one's functioning is fundamentally linked to events in nature and the elements of the universe
- *movement*–implies a premium placed on the interwoven mosaic of movement, dance, percussiveness, and rhythm personified by the musical beat
- *expressive individualism*–connotes the gleaning of uniqueness of personal expression, of style and of sincerity of expression. (Boykin & Ellison, 1995, pp. 99-100)

SOCIAL DEVELOPMENT AMONG AFRICANS

Prior to speculating on the potential relevance of the above dimensions for the social development of extant African-American youth, it seems prudent to consider briefly the social lives of African youth. Although contemporary African culture reflects the complex interweaving of African, European and Islamic traditions in increasingly urbanized societies, indigenous communal motifs are still foundational to the African experience (Gyekye, 1996; Nsamenang, 1992). Communalism is not inconsistent with what many cultural psychologists refer to as interdependence (e.g., Greenfield, 1994; Jagers & Mock, 1995; Markus & Kitayama, 1994). Simply put, communalism highlights collective concerns over individual rights and privileges. Within cross-cultural and cultural psychology communal cultures are typically contrasted with independent or individualistic cultures which give priority to personal rights and privileges.

The extended family is the quintessential expression of communalism, serving as the working model for all other social institutions (e.g., Davidson, 1969; Gyekye, 1996; Mbiti, 1970; Sudakarsa, 1988). It is critical to note, however, that the conduct of communal life has spiritual underpinnings. In this sense, the familial and other social networks extend both vertically and horizontally. The vertical vector is essentially a spiritual one–emphasizing one's connection with and responsibility to venerated ancestors (local and family-specific) and to future generations. This understanding informs relations along the horizontal vector which encompass both consanguineal and affinal kin. Thus, the fulfillment of social duties not only indicates an awareness of the shared vital essence of social others (Jagers & Smith, 1996), and commitment to collective well-being, but also demonstrates one's respect for past and future community members.

Although the development of children and youth is adult sponsored, other children play a central role in further inculcating and maintaining normative social behavior (Nsamenang, 1992; Turner, 1994). Community children are raised essentially as siblings, with youth spending the majority of their time in the company of their peers. In this context, the mentoring and monitoring of siblings and peers are an essential part of the social developmental process (Jahoda, 1982). Taken together, the influences of cultural agents (family, friends and community) intertwine and support each other. As such, they provide for relatively limited deviation from culturally desired developmental experiences and outcomes. This process is consistent with what has been termed narrow socialization (Arnett, 1995).

The transactions between cultural agents and youth are aimed primarily at the continued cultivation of "good character" in both parties (Gyekye, 1996; Nsamenang, 1992). Good character implies an ethical maturity evidenced by qualities which impact on others directly such as hospitality, generosity, justice, truthfulness and kindness (Menkiti, 1984). It also refers to self-focused qualities like contentment, moderation and perseverance (Gyekye, 1996). The latter constitute less observable, but clearly necessary qualities for sustained interdependence.

SOCIAL DEVELOPMENT AMONG AFRICAN-AMERICANS

This outline is not intended to paint African social life as idyllic. Surely, an unbiased examination of the cultural history of Africans or, for that matter, any group will reveal an array of societal limitations and inequities. What is intended, however, is to identify within this legacy those precepts and accompanying attitudes and behaviors which are available presently and could serve to enhance the collective quality of life. It appears that a systematic focus on spirituality, affect and communalism with an emphasis on their contributions to issues of character corresponds well with these aspirations.

Conceptually, it was reasoned that spirituality is evidenced among youth through a belief in the presence and guidance of deceased loved ones and/or a Supreme Being and a respect for God or the life force in social others. Affect is thought to be a mechanism through which one's spiritual endowment can be manifested and detected. An affective orientation denotes a valuing of emotional sincerity, an appreciation for the connections between feelings and thought, and a high regard for personal sentiment or opinion. Affective acuity is essential to the establishment and maintenance of communal relations. Among youth, communalism is reflected in an emphasis on social involvement, a willingness to assume social duties and a belief in cooperative relationships.

AN AFROCULTURAL SOCIAL ETHOS

Spiritual, affective and communal orientations each warrant and have received individual scholarly attention in research with adult and college age populations (e.g., Jagers & Mock, 1995; Jagers & Smith, 1996). However, we have asserted that considering these orientations in the aggregate holds significant promise as well. Our contention is that, taken together, these orientations form an Afrocultural social ethos (Jagers, 1996; Jagers, Smith, Mock & Dill, in press). This ethos reflects an awareness that genuine mutual interdependence is fostered through a recognition that a shared vital essence demands greater intra- and interpersonal sensitivity.

In our initial studies with inner-city youth grades 5-7 (e.g., Jagers &

Mock, 1993; Jagers, 1996, Jagers, Smith, Mock & Dill, in press), an Afrocultural social ethos and its component orientations of spirituality, affect and communalism tended to be positively endorsed, suggesting that many, but not all, youth resonated positively with the beliefs and behaviors presented. No gender differences in mean endorsements were detected. Such difference were expected since college age and adult women had significantly higher spirituality scores than did their male counterparts (Jagers et al., in press; Jagers & Smith, 1996). Among the youth, the moderately high positive correlations among the three orientations (e.g., .60) indicated that while each tended to be endorsed, they were not responded to as isomorphic phenomena.

It seems certain that families play a primary role in the degree to which youth acquire Afrocultural "modes, sequences and styles of behavior" (Boykin & Toms, 1985, p. 42). The literature on well-functioning inner-city families is replete with references to the importance of religious commitment and extended family functioning in helping such families and their children to thrive in spite of proximal and distal forces which would otherwise place them at serious risk (e.g., Billingsley, 1992; Harrison Wilson, Pine, Chan & Buriel, 1990; Jarrett, 1995; Taylor, Casten, & Flickinger, 1993; Staples & Johnson, 1993). Although this literature would seem to imply that families play an important role in youth's endorsement of an Afrocultural social ethos and related psychological characteristics, no direct examination of this thesis has been conducted.

Friendship relations represent a potentially fruitful avenue for exploring the influence of Afrocultural motifs in the lives of African-American youth since they play a crucial role in reinforcing and further honing social norms and practice among African youth. Unfortunately, the literature on peer relations and friendship among African-American youth is quite sparse. The literature which is available tends to feature a compensatory approach to peer relations (Giordano, Cenkovich & DeMaris, 1993). Specifically, it is widely assumed that, for low-income African-American youth, peers become surrogate parents early in life. It is also implied that resulting peer influences are inherently negative (e.g., Silverstein & Krate, 1975; Mason, Cauce, Gonzales & Hiraga, 1994).

However, some recent work contradicts this commonly held

view. For example, Giordano, Cenkovich and DeMaris (1993) have demonstrated that African-American youth, regardless of family income level, rely on family more than on peers for intimacy and guidance. Clark and Ayers (1994) reported that African-American youth do not necessarily place as much weight on similarity or reciprocity in their friendships as do their European-American counterparts. These findings may suggest that many African-American youth face lower levels of negative peer pressure than is typically assumed. However, left largely unexplored is the possibility that some friends have positive influences on each other. It seems reasonable to assume, for example, that youth whose friends embrace an Afrocultural social ethos would have experiences which promote desirable attitudes and behaviors.

Character as a Functional Consideration

Character formation and development are an important, yet understudied issue in the African-American community. The concept of character derives its relevance not only from a cursory review of African social life, but perhaps more importantly, from the myopic understanding of the social development of extant African-American youth, especially that of young men and boys. For example, although physical violence among young men is clearly one of the more salient and pressing problems facing urban communities (Hammond & Yung, 1993), only a small minority of young men in any given community actually engage in criminal or delinquent behaviors. While this subset of problem youth have garnered considerable publicity and substantial intellectual and material resources, very little is known about how and why similarly situated youth avoid problem or antisocial pursuits. Moreover, the myriad of instances of kindness, concern, and commitment which occur daily in the African-American community have not been the object of widespread systematic study. In essence, the normative social development of African-American youth has gone largely ignored.

The literature on character formation and development invites inquiry into an array of relevant psychological characteristics. For instance, Lickona (1991) equates good character with moral maturity. Moral maturity is constituted of moral knowing (e.g., self-knowledge, perspective-taking, moral reasoning), moral feeling (e.g., empathy, self-control, self-esteem) and moral action (e.g., competence, habit). Hay, Castle and Jewett (1994) offer a similar complement of psychological factors, but do not agree that these qualities are inherently moral in nature. They assert that character comprises six distinct but related components. These include: (1) empathic/sympathetic responding, (2) care of the young and needy, (3) a propensity for sharing, cooperation and fairness, (4) effective social problem solving and conflict resolution, (5) honesty and truthfulness, and (6) adherence to social conventions and moral norms.

Our work on the interface between cultural orientations and social functioning has included constructs which fall under the rubric of character. For example, an initial set of studies was concerned primarily with the role of cultural orientations in the problem behaviors of aggression and delinquency among inner-city youth. One aim of this research was to examine whether Afrocultural social ethos would mitigate against engaging in these problem behaviors. Findings from one study (Jagers & Mock, 1993) supported this position, revealing that higher endorsement of an Afrocultural as compared to an Anglocultural social ethos was associated with lower levels of self-reported aggression and delinquency among sixth graders. Although a follow-up study (Jagers, 1996) elucidated the positive contributions of Anglocultural orientations to these problem behaviors, the expectation that an Afrocultural social ethos (and its component orientations of spirituality, affect and communalism) would emerge as a negative predictor of such behavior was not supported. These inconsistent findings suggest a need for further inquiry into connections between an Afrocultural social ethos and externalizing problem behaviors. In addition, the internalizing behavior of social withdrawal warrants systematic attention. While social withdrawal can be problematic at extreme levels, in disenfranchised communities a certain amount of withdrawal might be adaptive, serving to minimize contact with those involved in undesirable activities (e.g., Jarret, 1995).

In other related work, we examined relationships between an Afrocultural social ethos and prosocial indicators among sixth and seventh graders (Jagers et al., in press). Greater endorsement of an Afrocultural social ethos was predictive of empathy, and of a more altruistic view of human nature. However, the anticipated positive relationship between an Afrocultural social ethos and peer ratings of prosocial behavior was not found. It was expected that there would be some continuity between social ethos, attitudes and behavior. One methodological limitation was the broad based nature of the prosocial behavior construct. Perhaps an improved operationalization would yield the expected relationship.

In sum, we have initiated a program of research which is concerned with issues of culture and social development among African-American youth. Within the Afrocultural realm of the African-American experience, we propose the systematic study of an Afrocultural social ethos. It was posited that family and friends are the primary conduits for the acquisition of this ethos. It was expected that the Afrocultural social ethos of family, friends and youth conjoin to forge aspects of good character in this population.

STUDY 1

Method

Participants. Ninety-three third and sixth grade students took part in this investigation. These children comprised all children in the two third grade and two sixth grade classrooms of a public elementary school. A total of 43 third graders (26 boys, 17 girls) and 50 sixth graders (21 boys, 29 girls) took part in the study. The school was 100% African-American with practically all children residing in a local high-rise public housing project. The sample was deemed to be low-income based on data indicating that a full 99% of students received free or reduced price lunches. A research team of African-American graduate and undergraduate students used whole class administration to gather the following data.

Measures and Procedures. The Afrocultural Questionnaire for Children is part of the Cultural Questionnaire for Children (CQC) (Jagers & Mock, 1993). The Afrocultural Questionnaire utilizes a series of nine vignettes to assess spirituality, affect and communalism in children and adolescents. Each vignette describes the attitudes and behaviors of a single actor. The gender of the actor varies across vignettes. Youth were asked to indicate the degree to which the actor is (1) "like your family members," (2) "like your friends," and (3) "like you." These queries were responded to on a four point rating scale ranging from 1 "not at all" to 4 "very much." A fourth item asked, "how do you like (the actor)." This item was responded to on a four point scale ranging from 1 "strongly dislike" to 4 "strongly like." An example of a communalism vignette is provided below.

> Roy feels that it is important to work for his family, friends and community. He feels best when he is doing things for friends and family rather than just for himself. He believes that what you do for others is more important than what you get out of it. The people Roy helps also help him.

As in previous work (Jagers et al., in press), the mean of the self (you) and preference ratings were used as orientation scores. The mean of youth's spiritual, affective and communal orientation scores were employed as an Afrocultural social ethos score. The measure has strong temporal stability (retest r = .81) after a two-week interval.

The aggression, delinquency and social withdrawal subscales of the *Child Behavior Checklist: Youth Self Report (YSR)* were administered (Achenbach & Edelbrock, 1987). Each construct is assessed using a gender-specific set of items. The items "I argue a lot," "I hang around with kids that get me in trouble," and "I keep from getting involved with others" represent common items of the aggression (alpha = .88), delinquency (alpha = .68), and social withdrawal (alpha = .71) subscales, respectively. All subscale items are responded to on a three-point scale ranging from 1 "not true" to 3 "very often true."

Results

Means for youth's Afrocultural social ethos (M = 3.02, SD =.48) and their perceptions of those of their family members (M = 2.95, SD = .61) and friends (M = 2.70, SD = .62) indicated that respondents felt that this ethos was at least somewhat reflective of themselves and their significant others. A series of ANOVAs yielded no significant grade or gender differences on these variables. Correlational analyses revealed youth's social ethos to be positively associated with their ratings of family member's ethos ($r = .64$, $p < .01$) and with ratings of friend's ethos ($r = .45$, $p < .01$).

No significant grade differences in aggression, delinquency or social withdrawal emerged. Attention was then turned to the prediction of these behaviors using gender, youth's social ethos, and ratings of family and friend's social ethos. As Table 1 shows, the model for aggressive behavior was statistically significant, $F (4,88) = 2.4$, $p < .05$ ($R^2 = .10$). Friends' social ethos emerged as a significant independent predictor, accounting for approximately 7% of the unique variance in aggression scores. The more friends were perceived as having an Afrocultural social ethos, the fewer aggressive behaviors youth reported.

A significant portion of the variance in delinquent behavior was explained by the model, $F (4, 88) = 3.60$, $p < .01$ ($R^2 = .14$). Gender and friends' social ethos emerged as significant independent predictors, accounting for 9% and 4% of the total variance, respectively. Boys reported more delinquent acts than did girls. Additionally, the higher the Afrocultural social ethos of one's friends, the fewer delinquent behaviors reported.

Similarly, the overall model accounted for a significant portion of the variance in social withdrawal scores, $F (4,88) = 4.98$, $p < .001$ ($R^2 = .19$). Gender again emerged as an independent predictor, accounting for 13% of the unique variance. Girls reported more social withdrawal than did boys. Further, the social ethos of family members was found to account for another 6% of the variance in social withdrawal scores. The greater the ethos of family, the more social withdrawal behaviors youth reported.

Discussion

In the present study, third and sixth grade girls and boys did not differ in their endorsement of an Afrocultural social ethos for themselves, their families, or their friends. Also, youth's social ethos was positively related to their perceptions of family and friends on this dimension. These variables and gender were used to predict self-reported aggressive, delinquent and social withdrawal behaviors. The gender differences in delinquency and social withdrawal were an-

TABLE 1. Standard Regression of Gender and Afrocultural Ethos Variables on Problem Behaviors

	Aggression			Delinquency			Social Withdrawal		
	R	Sr	Sr^2 Unique	R	Sr	Sr^2 Unique	R	Sr	Sr^2 Unique
Gender	.02	.03		-.29**	-.28**	.09**	.36***	.38***	.13***
Youth	.10	.06		-.04	-.03		.01	-.13	
Family	.18	.18		.07	.13	.	.17**	.23**	.06**
Friend	-.17**	-.26**	.07**	-.19*	-.20*	.04*	.02	-.01	
	R = .31			R = .38			R = .43		
	R^2 = .10			R^2 = .14			R^2 = .19		
	Adjusted R^2 = .06*			Adjusted R^2 = .10**			Adjusted R^2 = .15***		

* $p < .05$ ** $p < .01$ *** $p < .001$

ticipated. However, the relationships found to exist between the Afrocultural social ethos variables and the various problem behaviors were illuminating. Consistent with previous findings (Jagers, 1996), respondents' own social ethos did not emerge as an independent predictor of any of these behaviors. Instead, it appears that the ethos of friends is a key cultural factor in limiting youth's participation in externalizing behaviors. Such friends may create a more humanistic peer milieu in which interpersonal antagonism is frowned upon. On the other hand, it was determined that social withdrawal was stimulated by an Afrocultural family context. This family environment may prime youth to avoid or disengage from social situations which are deemed physically or psychologically threatening.

STUDY 2

Method

Participants. One hundred and one sixth and seventh graders participated in the study. The sample included all children in the two classrooms at each grade level at an inner-city public elementary school. There were 54 boys and 47 girls in the sample. The student body was judged to be low-income based on data showing that better than 90% of the children enrolled in the school received free or reduced price lunches. As in Study 1, a team of African-American graduate and undergraduate students used a whole class, read aloud procedure to achieve data collection. The youth were administered the following measures.

The *Afrocultural Questionnaire for Children* described above was also employed in Study 2. In addition, *Empathic Concern* and *Perspective Taking* were each assessed using items adapted from the seven item subscales developed by Davis (1983). Item analyses revealed that only three empathic concerns and four perspective taking items provided adequate internal consistency for inclusion in this study. Alpha coefficients of .66 and .75 were yielded for the empathic concern and perspective taking scales, respectively. "When I see someone being taken advantage of, I feel kind of protective towards them" is an example of an empathic concern item. The item "When I'm upset with someone, I usually try to put myself in his/her shoes for a while" is representative of items on the perspective taking measure. Items were responded to on a four point scale ranging from 1 "not at all like me" to 4 "very much like me."

Three Helping Behavior items were taken from a 25 item *Peer Nominated Social Competence* measure (Metropolitan Area Child Study, 1992). Youth were presented with lists of all of their classmates, which were divided by gender. As each item was read aloud, youth were asked to put a line through the name of each child who demonstrated the target behavior. For the present study, youth were asked to indicate the children "who like to share with others," "who help other kids," and "who do nice things to help other people."

Results

Overall, youth reported an Afrocultural social ethos to be somewhat reflective of them (M = 2.93, SD = .57), their family members (M= 2.89, SD = .66) and their friends (M = 2.57, SD = .65). There were no significant gender differences in the level of endorsement of these variables. Youth's social ethos was found to be positively associated both with their ratings of the social ethos of family members (r = .74, p < .01) and with that of friends (r = .28, p < .05).

Youth rated themselves as being somewhat prone to having empathetic concern for others and to take other's perspective. Peer ratings indicated that, on average, youth within a given classroom (approximately 25 students) were rated as demonstrating helping behaviors by four classmates.

Standard multiple regression procedures employed gender, youth's social ethos, and ratings of family members and friends' social ethos as predictors of empathic concern, social perspective taking and helping behavior. Table 2 displays the results of these analyses. As can be seen in Table 2, the overall model for empathic concern was significant, $F_{(4, 96)}$ = 8.84, p < .001, (R^2 = .33). Gender and ratings of family members emerged as significant independent predictors, accounting for 6% and 5% of the unique variance in these scores, respectively. Youth's social ethos approached statistical significance in this analysis.

A significant portion of the variance in perspective-taking scores also was explained , $F (4, 96) = 6.48$, $p < .001$, ($R^2 = .28$). Ratings of friends' social ethos emerged as a significant independent predictor, accounting for 6% of the unique variance explained. Again, youth's ethos approached, but did not reach, statistical significance.

The model for peer rated helping behavior was also statistically significant, $F (4, 96) = 7.81$, $p < .001$, ($R^2 = .30$). Gender emerged as the only independent predictor of these scores. Girls were more likely than boys to be nominated for helping behaviors, accounting for 22% of the total variance.

Discussion

Sixth and seventh grade boys and girls were similar in their endorsement of an Afrocultural social ethos for themselves, and their family and friends. The correspondence between the ethos of youth and that of their families was roughly three times that found for their friends. Interestingly, data suggested that perceptions of family and friends also held differential implications for the emotional and cognitive aspects of empathy among youth. An Afrocultural family milieu contributed to increased empathic concern, suggesting that such a family environment enhances a youth's sense of emotional connection. Girls were more inclined than boys to endorse this aspect of empathy as well. On the other hand, the ethos of friends was predictive of the propensity to take another's perspective. Although these findings suggested that these Afrocultural variables should inform helping behavior, no such relationship was found. Consistent with previous findings using a more general index of prosocial behavior (Jagers et al., in press), girls were seen by their classmates as being more helpful than were boys.

CONCLUSION

The Afrocultural realm of the African-American experience has not received adequate systematic attention. This research advanced

TABLE 2. Standard Regression of Gender and Afrocultural Ethos Variables on Prosocial Attitudes and Behavior

	Empathetic Concern			Perspective Taking			Helping Behavior		
	R	Sr	Sr² Unique	R	Sr	Sr² Unique	R	Sr	Sr² Unique
Gender	.25*	.24*	.06*	.17	.13	.04	.50***	.46***	.22***
Youth	.51	.20		.47	.23		.27	.06	
Family	.47*	.23*	.05*	.35	.05		.19	.12	
Friend	.08	−.06		.35*	.25*	.06*	−.11	−.17	
	R = .57 R² = .33 Adjusted R² = .29***			R = .53 R² = .28 Adjusted R² = .24***			R = .57 R² = .32 Adjusted R² = .29***		

*p < .05 **p < .01 ***p < .001

and examined the notion of an Afrocultural social ethos and its relevance to the development of good character among African-American children. Findings from two preliminary studies seem to bode well for this line of work. It was found that youth positively endorsed this ethos as representative of themselves, their families and friends. The absence of gender differences on the cultural variables was surprising. Specifically, it seemed reasonable to assume that sixth and seventh grade boys would find these more humanistic motifs less appealing for themselves and their friends than would their female counterparts. However, this assumption was not supported by the data.

The perception that family and friends embrace an Afrocultural social ethos was associated with positive endorsement of this ethos by respondents. Moreover, findings pointed to the specific functional implications of these two aspects of children's cultural phenomenology. For instance, although ethos had been found to be predictive of empathy (Jagers et al., in press), when placed together with perceptions of family and friends, an Afrocultural family milieu emerged as the factor which enhances children's emotional concern for others. Interestingly, such a family context also promotes keeping to one's self. This pattern may reflect the reality that children's concern for family members is reciprocated, while outside the family children must interact with people who may be hostile or indifferent to their well-being. It appears that children from Afrocultural families may make themselves less available to the possibility of being taken advantage of by such people.

Friends' social ethos promoted greater perspective taking. Moreover, such friends appear to minimize the frequency of aggressive and delinquent behaviors engaged in by youth. It may be that having friends with this more humanistic view serves a normative function, creating a peer context in which negative social behaviors are both unnecessary and unacceptable. Apparently, however, this mode of curtailing problem behaviors is not synonymous with the promotion of prosocial conduct. Gender, and not cultural variables, predicted peer-nominated helping behavior.

Future research will seek to employ multi-method strategies to delve further into the acquisition processes and the social functions of an Afrocultural social ethos. For instance, discussion of the Anglocultural and minority realms were intentionally minimized in this study. However, there is a need for in-depth exploration of the ways in which the three realms conflate with one another. This Afrographic approach (Boykin & Ellison, 1995; Jagers & Mock, 1993) is essential to describing existing cultural patterns in various communities. This tact also will better illuminate the important, yet poorly understood, connections between culture and race-related attitudes and behaviors.

In terms of cultural acquisition, the implications of the families' cultural inclinations and related variations in family roles, structures and dynamics for the development of boys and girls need to be fleshed out. Although there were relatively few gender differences found in the present studies, it is anticipated that a closer look at tacit and explicit familial messages and practices at various ages might unearth important gender-specific trends. Sibling relationships also need to be considered in this connection. Moreover, the present research strongly suggests the need for a culturally-informed analyses of how friendships are established and transacted at various ages. The developmental implications of friendship in the African-American community have not garnered much scholarly interest. Finally, analyses of cultural learning are incomplete without examining the contributions of the church, the school and the media.

The functional significance of Afrocultural and Anglocultural social ethos for social development warrants continued inquiry. The intersection of culture and issues of character is of particular interest in this regard. This nexus encompasses the study of morality which appears prominently in cultural psychology literature (e.g., Haidt, Keller & Dias, 1993; Miller & Bersoff, 1995; Shweder, 1991). However, much of the existing work compares European-Americans with foreign groups which, unlike African-Americans, are portrayed as culturally homogenous. The implications of this scholarship for understanding the moral cognitions, sensibilities and actions of African-Americans remains to be determined.

The need for increased self-sufficiency in the African-American community makes the distribution of resources and responsibility two of the more important areas of study. This research helps to shed light on such issues as cooperation, competition, sharing, need, entitlement, privilege, compassion, self-discipline, and sacrifice. Relatedly, research also is needed into social transgressions in the African-American community. For instance, how various forms of aggression and violence are understood and responded to warrants systematic attention. There are potentially important distinctions to be drawn between issues like self-assertion, instigation and retaliation. This invites consideration of corollary concerns such as self-regulation, guilt, shame, and reparations. Retributive justice and its component considerations of intentionality, harm, blame, punishment and forgiveness also present themselves as important points for inquiry.

This research agenda has clear implications for understanding children's emerging gender roles and notions of manhood. Culture provides the parameters within which gender identities and roles are constructed (Gilmore, 1990). For example, Oliver (1994) has proposed that the "tough guy" image is glorified among some inner-city African-American men. From the present view, this notion of manhood represents a contextualized adaptation of an Anglocultural social ethos (Jagers, 1996). The finding that boys, regardless of their Afrocultural social ethos, tended not to demonstrate helping behaviors may indicate the influence of this competing cultural agenda. Ucko (1994) has offered a similar analysis in attempting to understand elevated rates of conflict and violence in African-American male-female relations.

SOME PRACTICAL CONSIDERATIONS

A word about interventions seems appropriate here. Despite the sizable void in culturally-informed basic research, the need for immediate corrective action in the African-American community can not be ignored. In what follows, some of our tentative research findings are woven together with practical experiences with various community-based initiatives. The aim is to touch on some of the potential avenues and barriers to the healthy development of African-American boys and men.

Families are the first, and potentially the most influential forces in the lives of children. As such, they need to be supported in their child rearing efforts. School- and community-based interventions should endeavor to understand and to build on existing cultural inclinations and developmental imperatives families have for their young men. This strategy would increase their receptiveness and investment in the proposed intervention. This, in turn, would help to maximize program effectiveness. However, it is not clear that this collaborative tact is commonly employed. Most programmatic efforts continue to assume, either implicitly or explicitly, that African-Americans should be acculturated.

Youth who most need support typically come from families who are least prepared to assist and guide them. This is particularly true in cases where boys are not consistently exposed to and nurtured by a responsible adult male. It is intuitively appealing to suggest that more fortunate adults and peers could steer such boys and men toward a more appropriate life course. Despite the popularity of African proverbs like "It takes a village to raise a child," many community institutions and individuals have not effectively engaged the less fortunate or the misguided. For instance, although Black churches consistently provide spiritual and material sustenance to the faithful, many religious organizations have been unsuccessful in reaching the new generation of dispossessed who congregate just outside their doors (Quinn, 1994). Parents of well-prepared children living in poor communities work to psychologically distance themselves and their children from the less desirable element in the community (e.g., Jarrett, 1995). Other community residents are over-extended with work and family. Some have a rigid victim-blame view towards underachievers, while others are simply afraid of them. There are no ready remedies for these issues. Yet what is clear is that there exists a sizable number of boys and young men who are not adequately prepared, spiritually, intellectual, or socially. If they are to become caring, productive members of the community they need to first see and experience these qualities in others.

The Nguzo Saba (Karenga, 1980) is being employed increasingly to provide cultural grounding for school- and community-based programs and thus serve to mobilize indigenous community resources in the service of young men. Often thought of strictly in terms of the year-end celebration of Kwanzaa, the seven principles of the Nguzo Saba—unity (Umoja), self-determination (Kujichagu-

lia), collective work and responsibility (Ujima), cooperative eco-
nomics (Ujamaa), purpose (Nia), creativity (Kuumba), and faith
(Imani)–are actually intended to promote communal thought and
practice in daily dealings with one's family, community and racial
group. However, because many such programs are sponsored by the
socialist segment of the Black Nationalist community or liberal
European-Americans they often exclude or minimize issues of spirituality. Both groups have questions about the appropriateness and
utility of spirituality and religion. Thus, while notions of spirituality
continue to strike a harmonious cord among the masses of African-
American people, some initiatives fail to tap its potential as an
instrument of personal and social change.

Despite evidence that certain Afrocultural motifs will facilitate
desirable outcomes among African-American youth, it is inevitable
that youth have to negotiate contexts informed primarily by Anglocultural orientations. This is particularly true for school and work
environments. The possibility that certain Anglocultural motifs
contribute to problem outcomes (Jagers, 1996) makes it inappropri-
ate to encourage wholesale adoption or emulation of such motifs.
Instead, we advocate for a form of "reasoned biculturality" whereby an Afrocultural social ethos is supplemented with an instrumental understanding of useful Anglocultural orientations. This cultural
profile could be cultivated through a process of positional socialization (Lebra, 1994), which connotes increasingly complex instruction on the cultural repertoire expected and required in various
social contexts.

Of course, we encourage the careful, systematic evaluation of
any and all of these programmatic thrusts. For example, assessing
individual differences in cultural orientations might allow for a
better tailoring of programs to the cultural strengths and needs of
prospective participants. Further, there is a need to document
whether and in what ways programs and specific services are effective. Such knowledge facilitates retooling or fine-tuning programmatic efforts and provides for accurate replication or context-spe-
cific modifications. When used in this way, evaluative research
serves as a feedback mechanism for program activities. These systematic efforts are crucial to the process of adequately preparing our

youth for current and future challenges they will confront within family, community, national and global contexts.

REFERENCES

Achenbach, T.M. & Edelbrock, C. (1987). *Manual for the youth self-report and profile.* Burlington, VT: University of Vermont.

Arnett, J. (1995). Broad and narrow socialization: The family in the context of a cultural theory. *Journal of Marriage and the Family, 57,* 617-628.

Baldwin, J.A. (1991). African (black) psychology: Issues and synthesis. In R.L. Jones (Ed.), *Black psychology* (3rd edition), (pp. 125-135). Berkeley, CA: Cobb & Henry.

Berry, J.W., Poortinga, Y.H., Segall, M.H. & Dasen, P.R. (1992). *Cross-cultural psychology: Research and applications.* New York, NY: Cambridge University Press.

Betancourt, H., & Lopez, S.R. (1993). The study of culture, ethnicity and race in American psychology. *American Psychologist, 48,* 629-637.

Billingsley, A. (1992). *Climbing Jacob's ladder: The enduring legacy of African American families.* New York: Simon & Schuster.

Boykin, A.W. (1983). The academic performance of Afro-American children. In J. Spence (Ed.), *Achievement and achievement motives* (pp. 321-371). San Francisco: Freeman.

Boykin, A.W. (1993). Afrocultural integrity: Some conceptual and empirical vistas. Paper presented at the Biennial conference on the Psychocultural development of Black children. Washington, DC: Howard University.

Boykin, A.W. & Ellison, C.M. (1995). The multiple ecologies of Black youth socialization: An Afrographic analysis. In R.L. Taylor (Ed.), *African American youth: Their social and economic status in the United States* (pp. 93-128). Westport, CN: Praeger.

Boykin, A.W. & Toms, F. (1985). Black child socialization: A conceptual framework. In H.P McAdoo & J.L. McAdoo (Eds.), *Black children: Social, educational and parental environments* (pp. 33-52). Beverly Hills, CA: Sage.

Clark, M.L. & Ayers, M. (1994). Friendship similarity during early adolescence: Gender and racial patterns. *The Journal of Psychology, 126,* 393-405.

Davidson, D. (1969). *The African genius: An introduction to African social and cultural history.* Boston, MA: Little, Brown & Co.

Davis (1983). Measuring individual differences in empathy: Evidence for a multi-dimensional approach. *Journal of Personality and Social Psychology, 44,* 13-26.

Dei, G.J.S. (1994). Afrocentricity: A cornerstone of pedagogy. *Anthropology and Education Quarterly, 25,* 3-28.

DuBois, W.E.B. (1939). *Black folks, then and now.* New York: Holt.

Franklin, J.H. & Moss, A.A. (1988). *From slavery to freedom.* New York: Alfred A. Knopf.

Geertz, C. (1973). *Interpretations of cultures.* New York: Basic Books.

Gilmore, D. (1990). *Manhood in the making.* New Haven, CT: Yale University Press.

Giordano, P.C., Cenkovich, S.A. & Demaris, A. (1993). The family and peer relation of Black adolescents. *Journal of Marriage and the Family, 55,* 277-287.

Greenfield, P.M. (1994). Independence and interdependence as developmental scripts: Implications for theory, research and practice. In P.M. Greenfield and R.R. Cocking (Eds.), *Cross-cultural roots of minority child development* (pp. 1-37). Hillsdale, NJ: LEA.

Greenfield, P.M. & Cocking, R.R. (1994). *Cross-cultural roots of minority child development.* Hillsdale, NJ: LEA.

Gyekye, K. (1996). *African cultural values: An introduction.* Philadelphia, PA: Sankofa.

Haidt, J., Keller, S.M. & Dias, M.G. (1993). Affect, culture and morality, or is it wrong to eat your dog? *Journal of Personality and Social Psychology, 65,* 613-629.

Hammond, W.R. & Yung, B. (1993). Psychology's role in the public health response to assaultive violence among young African American men. *American Psychologist, 48,* 142-154.

Harrison, A.O., Wilson, M.N., Pine, C.J., Chan, S.Q. & Buriel, R. (1990). Family ecologies of ethnic minority children. *Child Development, 61,* 347-362.

Hay, D.F., Castle, J. & Jewett, J. (1994). Character development. In M. Rutter and D.F. Hay (Eds.), *Development through life: A handbook for clinicians* (pp. 319-349). Oxford: Blackell Scientific.

Herskovits, M.J. (1955). *Cultural anthropology.* New York: Alfred A. Knopf.

Herskovits, M.J. (1958). *The myth of the Negro past.* Boston: Beacon Press.

Holloway, J.E. (1990). *Africanisms in American culture.* Bloomington, IN: Indiana University Press.

Jagers, R.J. (1996). Culture and problem behaviors among inner-city African American youth: Further explorations. *Journal of Adolescence, 19,* 371-381.

Jagers, R.J. & Mock, L.O. (1995). The communalism scale and collectivist-individualistic tendencies: Some preliminary findings. *Journal of Black Psychology, 21,* 153-167.

Jagers, R.J. & Mock, L.O. (1993). Culture and social outcomes among inner-city African American children: An Afrographic analysis. *Journal of Black Psychology, 19,* 391-405.

Jagers, R.J. & Smith, P. (1996). Further examination of the Spirituality Scale. *Journal of Black Psychology, 22,* 429-442.

Jagers, R.J., Smith, P., Mock, L.O. & Dill, E. (in press). An Afrocultural social ethos: Component orientations, and some social correlates among inner-city youth. *Journal of Black Psychology, 24.*

Jahoda, G. (1982). *Psychology and anthropology: A psychological perspective.* London: Academic.

Jarrett, R. (1995). Growing up poor: The family experiences of socially mobile youth in low-income African American neighborhoods. *Journal of Adolescent Research, 10,* 111-135.

Jones, J.M.(1991). Racism: A cultural analysis of the problem. In R.L. Jones (Ed.), *Black psychology* (3rd edition), (pp. 609-635). Berkeley, CA: Cobb & Henry.

Karenga (1980). *Kawaida theory: An introductory outline.* Inglewood, CA: Kawaida Publications.

Lebra, T.S. (1994). Mother and child in Japanese socialization: A Japan-US comparison. In P.M. Greenfield and R.R. Cocking (Eds.), *Cross-cultural roots of minority child development* (pp. 259-274). Hillsdale, NJ: LEA.

Lickona, T. (1991). *Educating for character: How schools can teach respect and responsibility.* New York, NY: Bantam Books.

Markus, H. R. & Kitayama, S. (1994). The cultural construction of self and emotion: Implications for social behavior (pp. 89-132). In S. Kitayama and H.R. Markus (Eds.), *Emotion and culture: Empirical studies of mutual influence* (pp. 89-130). Washington, DC: American Psychological Association.

Mason, C.A., Cauce, A.M., Gonzales, N. & Hiraga, Y. (1994). Adolescent problem behavior: The effect of peers and the moderating role of father absence and the mother-child relationship. *American Journal of Community Psychology, 22,* 723-743.

Mbiti, J.S. (1970). *African Religions and Philosophy.* Garden City, NJ: Anchor.

Metropolitan Area Child Study (1992). University of Illinois at Chicago.

Menkiti, I.A. (1984). Person and community in African traditional thought. In R.A. Wright (Ed.), *African philosophy: An introduction* (pp. 171-182). Lanham, MD: University Press of America.

Miller, J.G. & Bersoff, D.M. (1995). Development in the context of everyday family relationships: Culture, interpersonal relationships and adaptation. In M. Killer and D. Hunt (Eds.), *Morality in everyday life* (pp. 259-282). Cambridge: Cambridge University Press.

Myers, L.J. (1991). Expanding the psychology of knowledge optimally: The importance of worldview revisited. In R.L. Jones (Ed.), *Black psychology* (3rd edition), (pp. 15-28). Berkeley, CA: Cobb & Henry.

Nobles, W.W. (1991). *African philosophy: Foundations of black psychology.* In R.L. Jones (Ed.), *Black psychology* (3rd edition), (pp. 47-64). Berkeley, CA: Cobb & Henry.

Nsamenang (1992). *Human development in cultural context: The third world perspective.* Newbury Park, CA: Sage.

Oliver, W. (1984). Black males and the tough guy image: A dysfunctional compensatory adaptation. *The Western Journal of Black Studies, 8,* 199-203.

Oliver (1994). *The violent social world of Black men.* New York, NY: Lexington Books.

Quinn, J. (1994). Traditional youth support systems and their work with young Black males. In R. Mincy (Ed.), *Nurturing young Black males: Challenges to agencies, programs, and social policy* (pp. 119-162). Washington, DC: Urban Institute Press.

Shweder, R.A. (1991). *Thinking through cultures: Expeditions in cultural psychology.* Cambridge, MA: Harvard University Press.

Silverstein, E. & Krate, R. (1975). *Children of the dark ghetto: A developmental psychology.* New York: Praeger.

Staples, R. & Johnson, L.B. (1993). *Black families at the crossroads: Challenges and prospects.* San Francisco: Jossey-Bass.

Stuckey, S. (1987). *Slave culture: Nationalist theory and the foundation of Black culture.* New York: Oxford University Press.

Sudarkasa, N. (1988). Interpreting the African heritage in Afro-American family organization. In H.P. McAdoo, (Ed.), *Black families (2nd edition)* (pp. 27-43).

Taylor, R.L. (1991). Poverty and adolescent Black males: The subculture of disengagement. In P.B. Edelman and J. Ladner (Eds.), *Adolescence and poverty: Challenge for the 1990's* (pp. 139-161). Washington, DC: Center for National Policy Press.

Taylor, R.D., Casten, R. & Flickinger, S.M. (1993). Influence of kinship support on parenting experiences and psychological adjustment of African American adolescents. *Developmental Psychology, 29,* 382-388.

Thompson, R.F. (1983). *Flash of the spirit: African and Afro-American art and philosophy.* New York: Vintage Books.

Triandis, H. (1972). *The analysis of subjective culture.* New York: Wiley.

Turner, V. (1994). "Growing" girls into women and "making" boys into men. In H.T. Neve (Ed.), *Homeward journey: Readings in African studies,* (pp. 135-138). Trenton, NJ: African World Press.

Ucko, C.Q. (1994). Culture and violence: Interaction of Africa and America. *Sex Roles, 31,* 185-294.

Woodson, C.G. (1968). *The African background outlined.* New York: Negro Universities Press.

Managing Anger:
Protective, Proactive, or Adaptive Racial Socialization Identity Profiles and African-American Manhood Development

Howard C. Stevenson

University of Pennsylvania

SUMMARY. African-American male risk and resilience is viewed as two sides of the same coin in this study that investigates the stability of cluster profiles of racial socialization beliefs. Responses of 208 urban African-American adolescent males from three different samples were used to empirically derive factors of spiritual/religious coping, extended family caring, cultural pride reinforcement, and racial awareness, which were then submitted to exploratory and confirmatory cluster analyses. Three reliable clusters were found across the samples and were identified as protective, proactive, and adaptive racial socialization beliefs. One-way ANOVAs were conducted on each sample separately and then combined with various psychosocial variables including anger expression, depression, religiosity, calamity fears, and kinship social support. The results supported the hypothesis that young males who hold an adaptive or proactive racial socialization identity tend to demonstrate more prosocial adjustment outcomes. The implications for prevention and community services are suggested. *[Article copies available for a fee from The Haworth Document Delivery Service: 1-800-342-9678. E-mail address: getinfo@haworth.com]*

[Haworth co-indexing entry note]: "Managing Anger: Protective, Proactive, or Adaptive Racial Socialization Identity Profiles and African-American Manhood Development." Stevenson, Howard C. Co-published simultaneously in *Journal of Prevention & Intervention in the Community* (The Haworth Press, Inc.) Vol. 16, No. 1/2, 1997, pp. 35-61; and: *Manhood Development in Urban African-American Communities* (ed: Roderick J. Watts, and Robert J. Jagers) The Haworth Press, Inc., 1997, pp. 35-61. Single or multiple copies of this article are available for a fee from The Haworth Document Delivery Service [1-800-342-9678, 9:00 a.m. - 5:00 p.m. (EST). E-mail address: getinfo@haworth.com].

The psychosocial adjustment of African-American male youth has been under scrutiny and question and there are increasing volumes on this topic (Majors & Billson, 1992; Majors & Gordon, 1994). The explanations for aberrant behaviors in Black male youth have ranged from genetic to environmental possibilities, but primarily these explanations have promoted a negative orientation to Black manhood development (Stevenson, 1992). The "endangered species" label, although used less recently, is implied when statistics regarding jail, probation, and parole status figures are coupled with homicide rates of Black young men (Gibbs, 1988). Despite the prevalence of deficit psychological orientations toward Black male promise and proficiency, there is a rising tide of research and intervention models that appreciate the phenomenological experiences of these youth (Cauce & Gonzales, 1993; Spencer, 1995; Stevenson, in press-a).

Racial socialization processes, measurement, and interventions have received significant attention within the last three years and promise to be a major dynamic in understanding and explaining the psychological adjustment and identity development of African-American and other families and youth of color (Boykin & Toms, 1985; Stevenson, 1994). Racial socialization is a concept that describes the process of communicating, receiving, and believing verbal and nonverbal messages and behaviors that shape one's sense of identity across the lifespan. Such socialization includes both racially oppressive and empowering encounters. This construct has been applied to the parenting of toddlers and children (Marshall, 1995; Peters, 1985), adolescents (Bowman & Howard, 1985; Stevenson, 1994b), as well as to the perceptions of racial socialization by the elderly (Thornton, Chatters, & Allen 1990).

Some distinction must be made between the meaning of ethnic or cultural and racial socialization although the overlap between these dynamics are integrated. Often race and culture are used to mean the same phenomenon while ethnic socialization and racial socialization are meant to describe the same process. In this work, racial socialization denotes the processes of child-rearing techniques and messages that are about one's racial makeup, one's social status, one's physical presentation to American society. Race is a socially constructed idea that has reference to a biological classification system and one's African physical presentation is often what initiates socially oppressive or culturally empowering encounters. In contrast, ethnicity and culture are synonymous and refer to values, practices, and learned behaviors (e.g., language, religion, and custom) that are shared commonly among persons within an existing group and that are transmitted across generations. Ethnicity and culture (and the socialization strategies that accompany them) are broader than racial socialization strategies, as defined by the literature. While the erroneous and implicit over-reliance upon one's physical appearance as the means for judging African-American ability and promise is not supported, it is evident that issues of skin color (and how others perceive persons of African descent) are primarily responsible for the concern by many African-American parents that their children are in need of buffering from American racial ambivalence and disdain. Prejudicial attitudes certainly exist toward persons who are ethnically or culturally different (often among persons within the same racial grouping which has been referred to as "colorism," see Njeri, 1993 and Stevenson & Abdul-Kabir, 1996), the experience of racism does not usually lend itself to such deeper distinctions of cultural values. It is the physical presentation that often invokes certain encounters that give cause to the role of racial socialization practices. The overlay of gender for African-American parents complicates matters as many believe their male children are targets of hostility for being Black and male.

Other characteristics of being African-American more adequately fit within the classifications of culture and ethnicity (e.g., interpersonal interaction, gender development, and language styles) and also contribute to members in society making determinations about one's racial status. These dynamics are important to our discussion but are not necessarily the focus of quantitative investigations of racial socialization. Ethnographic studies of socialization are better at identifying their impact (Stevenson & Abdul-Kabir, 1996). Boykin and Toms (1985) have identified three distinct family socialization patterns among African-American families. Those orientations include mainstream, minority, and Afrocultural styles. This classification fits more succinctly within a cultural or ethnic socialization framework and less adequately within a racial socialization framework, although the overlap makes studying this area very challenging.

Cultural socialization models help to explain more fully the context of behaviors for many urban African-American youth as well as prescribe different strategies for improving the psychological adjustment and behaviors of male teens (Boykin & Ellison, 1995; Heath, 1995). A cultural socialization model is proposed here in contrast to solely a racial socialization model since gender, ethnicity, sexual orientation, and racial development are combinations of key identity processes that are more accurately subsumed as "cultural." Race is to culture as orange is to color. A racial socialization framework tends to see race as the whole or outer shell of an individual while a cultural framework views race as one of many aspects of the individual. One model that appreciates the interrelationship of cultural, ecological, individual, and societal factors is the Phenomenological Variant on Ecological Systems Theory by Margaret Spencer and her colleagues (Spencer, 1995). This model acknowledges Bronfenbrenner's (1989) ecological systems theory but introduces the meaning-making experiences of youth of color as a central factor in understanding the relative impact of high-risk environments on these youth. This shift implies an appreciation of process within the person and context interaction and allows for the individual's perception and experience of sex role and racial stereotypes and biases to be considered within the research across five components. Within Spencer's model, *risk factors* include one's appraisal of stereotypic and biased reactions to one's race, socioeconomic status, gender, physical status, and neighborhood volatility. These risk factors are mediated by *stress engagement experiences,* that is, one's perceptions, experiences, and buffers of stress, which in turn impact upon the *coping methods* of youth (e.g., maladaptive and adaptive). From these coping methods, one's *identity* or persona emerges and contributes to life choices and behaviors that lead to *life outcomes.* This work is remarkable in that the phenomenological experiences of youth can be identified at each level of risk factor, stress engagement, coping strategy, identity development, and life stage outcome. Identifying the relationship between societal conditions and individual psychological coping is a creative new sensitivity to stress, cultural resources, and context factors that has eluded social science researchers for decades when studying the identity coping of African-American youth. Major themes of Dr. Spencer's work are that African-American male identity development involves competently making meaning of context (including the negative assumptions attributed to skin color and racial status), that multiple outcomes can occur for individuals from the same context, and that cultural socialization can promote healthy outcomes.

Building on Spencer's earlier work on the cultural transmission of values (1990), Stevenson (1994a) has proposed that racial and cultural socialization processes are necessary in order for African-American children, adolescents, and families to become psychologically healthy in a racially hostile society. Furthermore, he has suggested that understanding socialization processes from the adolescent's phenomenological experience is essential to measuring (qualitatively as well as quantitatively) the influence of cultural transmission on psychological and behavioral outcomes. Stevenson and colleagues have studied two different angles regarding adolescent perspectives on racial socialization–beliefs and experiences.

RACIAL SOCIALIZATION THEORY PROPOSITIONS

While a model or theory of racial socialization is yet to be established, several theoretical considerations promote a valid racial socialization measurement and intervention model from an adolescent perspective (Stevenson, in press). Stevenson (in press-b) has identified five ways one might approach the assessment of racial socialization between parents and adolescents. Four of these family context approaches encompass adolescent and parental *beliefs* and *experiences* about racial socialization processes. The fifth approach involves a matching or correspondence between parental communications and adolescent experiences, that is, what parents say they give to their children and what their children report as receiving. *Beliefs* are distinguished from experiences in that beliefs represent a communal self identity perspective or the perception of the other that reflects the self identity, while *experiences* represent our reporting of interactions with parenting. Beliefs fit more within the theoretical framework of symbolic interactionism where the generalized other is core to the definition of the self (Burke, 1993; Lal, 1995; Mead, 1956). Beliefs are essentially attitudes about interaction processes that lead to certain identity statuses. This is why within an African-centered perspective, racial socialization beliefs are more akin to the identity attitude research of Cross, Parham, and Helms (1991). Racial socialization beliefs are measured by asking the adolescent respondent his or her agreement (e.g., five point Likert-type scale) with a statement about how African-American parents should raise their children in a particular way (e.g., Scale of Racial Socialization Attitudes–for Adolescents–SORS-A). In essence, this practice is different from the Nigrescence theory-based Racial Identity Attitude Scale (RIAS) because the student is asked to respond "with his or her people or community in mind." This is where an extended self perspective is salient in the test design and administration of the SORS-A. Other socially interactional models of identity development are being constructed (Oyserman, Gant, & Ager, 1995).

In contrast, a person-environment and stress management theoretical orientation (Kaminoff & Proshansky, 1982; Pearlin, 1982; Peterson & Spiga, 1982) most aptly captures the understanding of racial socialization experiences (Stevenson, Herrero-Taylor, & Cameron, in press). Experiences are measured differently than beliefs and ask the respondent to report the frequency of racially socializing interactions and messages received from caregivers. Research on beliefs and experiences have led to the hypothesis that racial socialization perspectives can be measured and found to influence how teenagers psychologically adjust to societal animosity toward their social status as persons of color (Stevenson, 1994b; 1995; Stevenson, in press; Stevenson, Cameron, & Herrero-Taylor, in press; Stevenson, Herrero-Taylor, & Cameron, in press; Stevenson, Reed, & Bodison, in press).

Stevenson (1994b) conducted a validation study on the SORS-A and found four factors and two underlying themes of proactive and protective racial socialization identity beliefs for adolescents. Protective racial socialization beliefs view the world as racially hostile and worthy of distrust, encourage youth to discern supportive or hostile racial intentions, take on a tone of caution, and encourage youth to succeed despite external oppression. Proactive racial socialization beliefs encourage the individual to succeed as a function of internal talent, cultural heritage, and pays less attention to external oppression. Proactive beliefs are focused more intensively on the respondent's endorsement of parental strategies that instill a sense of cultural empowerment in youth.

Stevenson (1994b) found that proactive racial socialization beliefs consisted of three factors: spiritual and religious coping (SRC), cultural pride reinforcement (CPR), and extended family caring (EFC); while protective racial socialization beliefs consisted of one factor: racism awareness teaching (RAT). Adolescents who were high in proactive racial socialization beliefs were more likely to score high on the internalization scale of the Black Racial Identity Attitudes Scale (RIAS) while those who were high in protective racial socialization beliefs were more likely to reject a pre-encounter worldview that denied the salience of race in interpersonal and political affairs. Both types of racial socialization beliefs were essential in promoting psychologically mature racial identity outcomes according to Nigrescence theory. Gender differences with respect to the impact of racial socialization justified the investigation of male and females separately. For example, African-American males with higher levels of CPR showed fewer experiences of situational anger and outward physical or verbal anger. A higher degree of endorsement of EFC resulted in higher levels of reported anger control in males. Conversely, protective racial socialization beliefs tended to be positively related to decreased anger control and greater anger suppression in males. These significant findings point to a gender-specific orientation toward the internalization of cultural socialization and may point to the different styles in which African-American boys and girls are socialized with regard to gender and racial identity.

Currently, no study has investigated whether an integration of proactive and protective racial socialization beliefs are related to psychologically healthy outcomes in African-American male youth. This author would characterize this integration as "adaptive." One theoretical proposition is that proactive *and* protective racial socialization beliefs are necessary for promoting healthy psychosocial outcomes and in helping the individual survive and overcome racial antagonism in healthy ways (Stevenson, 1994a; 1994b; Stevenson,

Reed, & Bodison, in press). It is hypothesized that young men described as holding an adaptive or integrated racial socialization identity perspective will demonstrate healthier psychological outcomes than those with either protective or proactive perspectives alone. That is, one must be aware of racial hostility but not become consumed by it and eventually seek to orient his or her life around it. It is further proposed that a proactive perspective may yield better psychological outcomes than a protective orientation, primarily because of the restraint of societal intolerance for difference within a racially embattled context. Within an African psychological perspective, a balance of perspectives is encouraged, but no one perspective is inherently pathological (James-Myers, 1991; Nobles, 1991). One way to test out whether such identity orientations (e.g., proactive, protective, or adaptive) exist is to use a cluster analytic technique on several samples of African-American male youth. It must be determined if these identity statuses are consistent across different samples and if they are reliable.

In summary, this study seeks to identify distinct identity profiles from a racial socialization perspective, analyze their integrity, and to verify the existence of those profiles across varying samples. Furthermore, the research will analyze relationships of these identity statuses to various psychosocial outcomes to support or modify a theory of racial socialization identity that integrates proactive and protective aspects of interracial problem solving for African-American adolescent males.

METHOD

Participants

The 204 male participants in this study were derived from three studies, each of which focused on the psychosocial adjustment of African-American youth. Each study was conducted over a five month period, within a five year research program designed to understand the connection of racial socialization factors to the life coping strategies of African-American teenagers. Initially, each sample was analyzed using a K-means cluster analytic strategy to investigate the presence of proactive, protective, and adaptive identity statuses. The following measures were present in all three studies.

Measures

Scale of Racial Socialization (SORS-A). The SORS-A (Stevenson, 1994b) is a 45-item measure composed of five factors, that investigates adolescents' personal opinions about socialization activities with children in African-American families. Internal consistency of the total scale score of the SORS-A are adequate (alpha = .75; M = 170.1, SD = 16.2). Previous research revealed that a four factor model derived from a five factor solution was the most meaningful for interpretation of the SORS-A (Stevenson, 1994b). Factor 1 is called *Spiritual and Religious Coping* (SRC) and includes items that represent messages about recognizing spirituality and religion as helpful to surviving life's experiences (M = 26.8, SD = 4.9, alpha = .74). Factor 2 is called *Extended Family Caring* (EFC) and includes items that express attitudes and interactions that promote the role of extended and immediate family as serving child rearing and caring functions (M = 44.4, SD = 5.9; alpha = .70). Factor 3 represents items and attitudes that endorse the teaching of African-American history, culture, and pride to children and is entitled *Cultural Pride Reinforcement* (CPR; M = 27.7, SD = 4.3; alpha = .63). Factor 4 is called *Racism Awareness Teaching* (RAT) and is a subscale of items that focus on messages and attitudes that promote cautious and preparatory views regarding the presence of racism in society and the need to discuss racism openly among all family members (M = 38.8, SD = 6.7; alpha = .62).

State-Trait Anger Expression Inventory (STAXI). The STAXI (Spielberger, 1988) is a 44 item measure of the experience and expression of anger. It is comprised of seven subscales, three of which correspond to the experience of anger and four that correspond to the expression of anger. The anger experience subscales include state anger which are relatively intense angry feelings at a particular time. Trait anger is made up of two subscales, temperamental trait anger and reactive trait anger. Temperamental trait anger is the disposition to experience and express anger without specific provocation, while reactive trait anger is the disposition to experience and express anger when criticized or treated unfairly by other individuals. Four subscales constitute the expression of anger including anger-in, anger-out, anger-con, and anger expression. Anger-in represents anger suppression and the degree to which angry feelings are experienced but held in. Anger-out is the degree to which an individual expresses physical anger toward other people or objects in one's environment. Anger-con is the degree to which one is able to control angry outbursts. Anger expression is a general index of the frequency that anger is expressed, regardless of direction. Cronbach's alphas for the subscales ranged from .70 to .95. Spielberger (1988) has demonstrated competent reliability and validity statistics on this measure for adolescents from diverse backgrounds. In this model, healthier responses include lower levels of temperamental and reactive anger, suppressed anger, overt anger, and frequency of anger expression and moderate levels of anger control. Several studies have highlighted the detrimental physical and psychological outcomes for Black adolescent males with anger problems (Johnson, 1989, 1990; Johnson, 1991; Jones, Peacock, & Christopher, 1992).

Multi-Score Depression Index (MDI). The MDI (Berndt, 1986) is a well-researched measure of several indices of variables associated with overall depression. The subscales of the MDI include guilt, sad mood, irritability, low self-esteem, instrumental helplessness, social introversion, low energy, and pessimism. The 47 item short form was used for the 1993 sample, Study 1, which includes all of the subscales except learned helplessness. Berndt (1989) has conducted extensive research and scale alpha reliabilities range from .70 to .98. The long form of the MDI was used in Sample 2.

Kinship Social Support. The Kinship Social Support Scale (KSS) is a 13 item measure developed by Taylor, Casten, and Flickinger (1993) and was used in Samples 1 and 3. It measures the adolescent's perceptions of the amount of social and emotional support that their families receive from adult relatives in the areas of problem solving, socialization, entertainment, and advice. Taylor et al. (1993) found that there was adequate internal consistency to the instrument with alpha = .72. Kinship Social Support was divided into low (scores of 39 and below), medium (scores between 40 and 44), and high (scores of 45 and above) levels by using the 33rd and 66th percentiles as the cutoff scores. The internal consistency of the

KSS was supported for the current study. The KSS was found to have a reliability coefficient of .75, with a mean score of 41.1 (range from 25 to 52) and a standard deviation of 5.8.

Fear of Calamity Scale. A measure of negative urban life experiences was designed by the author specifically for this study and is based on three years of interviewing teenagers regarding their fears about surviving urban neighborhoods. This is a six item measure including fears of getting shot, getting stabbed, getting AIDS, getting beat up, getting sick, and dying young. Reliability analyses reveal Cronbach's alpha of .78.

Several basic demographic and psychosocial questions were asked across all three samples. Those questions included composite questions about religiosity (e.g., extrinsic church attendance and intrinsic spiritual orientation to the world), mother and father's educational level, and how many persons are currently living in the home.

Sample 1

This sample consisted of 93 African-American teenage males and the research was conducted in 1992. The central psychosocial variables in this study included Nigrescence Theory identity statuses, church attendance and spirituality, and aspects of depression. The primary hypotheses involved identifying a positive relationship between racial socialization and racial identity and an inverse relationship between racial socialization beliefs and depression. The primary measure used in this study was the Racial Identity Attitude Scale (RIAS).

Racial Identity Attitude Scale. The Racial Identity Attitude Scale is a measure with adequate psychometric properties including reliability and validity (Ponterotto & Wise, 1987). The 50 item version was utilized with Sample 1. The RIAS was analyzed according to the four stages of Nigrescence–Pre-encounter, encounter, Immersion/Emersion, and internalization. Given that very few studies have administered this instrument to young adolescents, a principal components analysis was conducted. Following a review of the scree plot and the item loadings, three salient factors were identified and corresponded to three of the four Nigrescence theory stages (i.e., excluding encounter). The factors, Pre-encounter ($M = 21.1$,

SD = 5.4, Range = 10-44, Median = 20, 10 items), immersion (M = 27.3, SD = 5.4, Range = 15-45, Median = 27.5, 11 items), and internalization (M = 54.6, SD = 7.8, Range = 28-70, Median = 55.0, 16 items) are so-named because the items match very well the original factors, according to the Parham and Helms measure (1990). These factors account for 22% of the variance of the construct and an orthogonal varimax rotation yielded meaningful results that held consistent with other factor analytic strategies including quartermax and oblimin rotations. Both orthogonal and nonorthogonal strategies were utilized because of the questions within the Nigrescence literature about the continuous or disjunctive relationship between the stages (Helms, 1991). If the stages are continuous then their intercorrelations should be moderate. The factors demonstrated internal consistency with alpha coefficients of .61, .67, and .77, for pre-encounter, immersion, and internalization, respectively.

Sample 2

The second sample of 41 males was drawn from Stevenson et al. (in press). This work attempted to identify relationships among racial socialization beliefs, HIV/AIDS prevention beliefs, sexual behavior, and psychological adjustment of African-American youth. Only the data on racial socialization and anger expression will be used for this article. The primary measures used for this study included the SORS-A and the STAXI.

Sample 3

In this sample of 74 males, two measures were added to test the hypotheses that adolescent racial socialization beliefs and experiences were related to the psychological adjustment of youth. A new measure called the Teenager Experience of Racial Socialization (TERS) was developed (Stevenson, Cameron, & Herrero-Taylor, in press). This measure presupposes proactive and protective aspects to parenting strategies in families of color, in particular African-American families. The items were written to be as clear and behavioral as possible and ask the respondent to tell how much he or she has received racial socialization communications or interactions.

The response format is a three point frequency format (e.g., never, a few times, lots of times). Specific goals of the TERS in comparison to the SORS-A includes: (1) to increase the reliability of the factors and the entire measure by specifying clear, behavioral examples of racial socialization practice; (2) to further the understanding of family socialization interactions from an adolescent's perspective; and (3) to better capture the frequency of racial socialization messages without relying upon simple yes or no responses.

A factor analysis of the TERS revealed four factors. Factor 1, *Cultural Survival Socialization* (CSS), includes items that represent messages about the maintenance of African-American cultural heritage and the importance of struggling successfully through racial hostilities. Factor 2 is called *Racism Struggles Socialization* (RSS). It includes items about messages about the barriers of racism in society and overcoming those barriers. Factor 3 represents items and attitudes that endorse the teaching of pride and knowledge of African-American culture to children and is entitled *Pride Development Socialization* (PDS). Factor 4, *Spiritual Coping Socialization* (SRC), reflects messages about the role of spirituality and religious involvement as helpful in coping with life and race struggles.

Cronbach's alpha for the entire TERS scale (e.g., Global Racial Socialization Experience) was .84 (n = 178). The mean for the total scale was 91.2 ($SD = 10.7$). The reliability for most of the factors is moderate and above an alpha of .74 (Spirituality Coping Socialization, alpha = .76; $M = 15.5$, $SD = 3.4$; Cultural Survival Socialization, alpha = .73, $M = 23.2$, $SD = 4.3$; Pride Development Socialization, alpha = .76, $M = 19.5$, $SD = 2.3$; Racism Struggles Socialization, alpha = .74, $M = 18.4$, $SD = 3.6$). *Family Discussion About Racism* is a single question about how often one's family discusses discrimination. It asked "How much does your family talk about racism and discrimination?" The respondent could choose from five likert-type responses ranging from "Not Much" to "All of the Time."

RESULTS

In each analysis, the three proactive racial socialization factors of SRC, CPR, and EFC and the one protective racial socialization beliefs factor of RAT were included for each sample. One-way ANOVAs, corrections, and Scheffe post-hoc tests were again conducted within each of the three studies and the aggregated sample to determine the relationship between the identified clusters and the specific psychosocial variables of each study. Finally, all three samples were aggregated as a way to facilitate and confirm the reliability of the identified cluster profiles.

After investigating all three data sets, a three cluster solution was identified and was confirmed to be the most meaningful. The three clusters meaningfully fit within the three categories of proactive (Proact), protective (Protect), and adaptive (Adapt) racial socialization beliefs. The determination of cluster definition rested upon the following criteria. To be defined as a Proact cluster, the cluster would have to demonstrate at least a .5 standard deviation between proactive SORS-A factors (e.g., SRC, EFC, and CPR) and the protective SORS-A factor (e.g., Racism Awareness Teaching-RAT). The Protect cluster was defined as a cluster having RAT as the highest SORS-A factor among all factors and demonstrating at least a .5 standard deviation separation from the RAT factor. The Adaptive cluster was defined as having all four SORS-A factors (e.g., RAT, SRC, EFC, and CPR) as being separated by no more than .5 standard deviation in z-score. Table 1 displays the means of racial socialization clusters across the three samples.

The internal consistency reliability and validity of the three clusters were ascertained in a number of ways. First, the reliability of the SORS-A variables was explored using a criterion of .65, a criterion deemed adequate for measures of psychosocial adjustment. Secondly, the validity of a cluster solution was determined by investigating whether the same clusters could be replicated across different data sets. Third, validity was assessed by performing significance tests that compare the clusters on variables *not* used to generate the cluster solution (Aldernderfer & Blashfield, 1984); in this case, the variables were psychological adjustment variables.

Reliability

First, cluster reliabilities were conducted by data-set. For Samples 1-3, the internal consistency reliabilities were .67, .80, and .70, respectively. For the data set combining all three samples, the reli-

TABLE 1. Means of Racial Socialization Clusters Profiles Across Three Samples

	Spiritual Religious Coping	Extended Family Caring	Cultural Pride Reinforce.	Racism Awareness Teaching
Sample 1				
Racial Socialization Clusters				
1. Protective (n = 18)	22.7	34.7	26.7	37.3
2. Proactive (n = 20)	29.8	48.5	35.0	32.2
3. Adaptive (n = 45)	25.8	46.2	32.0	43.5
Sample 2				
1. Protective (n = 4)	17.8	24.3	17.5	34.3
2. Proactive (n = 20)	29.3	45.4	34.4	34.9
3. Adaptive (n = 17)	23.2	42.3	30.4	31.3
Sample 3				
1. Protective (n = 14)	21.5	35.1	27.0	36.3
2. Proactive (n = 40)	29.1	43.6	32.1	30.9
3. Adaptive (n = 20)	26.2	45.8	35.3	36.5
Combined Samples 1-3				
1. Protective (n =36)	21.6	33.6	25.7	35.6
2. Proactive (n = 102)	28.6	45.1	33.4	31.4
3. Adaptive (n = 70)	25.8	45.9	32.5	42.2

ability coefficient was .72. Second, a correlation analysis between single and combined data-set cluster membership was conducted. By assigning a single data set cluster membership to each case and a combined data set cluster membership, each case holds two cluster membership scores and the strength of the relationship between both memberships was determined. A correlation score of .72 (p < .0001) was found which indicates a high degree of assurance that each case held the same cluster membership across single and combined data sets. The third step in determining validation for the three clusters involved identifying discriminating but significant relationships between the three clusters on external variables, and across all three data sets. Table 1 provides the means of the Racial

Socialization subscale scores for each cluster across all three samples.

Sample 1

ANOVAs between the clusters for each SORS-A factor revealed that all three clusters differed significantly (SRC: $F = 17.3$, $p < .0001$; CPR: $F = 27.0$, $p < .0001$; EFC: $F = 64.9$, $p < .0001$; RAT: $F = 47.6$, $p < .0001$). With respect to how much African-American males use spirituality to govern their lives, an overall F score of 2.59 approached significance ($p < .08$). Using Scheffe's post-hoc tests, Proactive young men were significantly more spiritually minded than young men from the Adaptive cluster. The Adaptive cluster was found to be higher than either the Protective or Proactive clusters in feelings of guilt ($F = 3.70$, $p < .05$) and higher than the Proactive cluster in feelings of instrumental helplessness ($F = 2.97$; $p < .05$). With respect to Black Racial Identity and the Cross theory of Nigrescence, African-American males in the Protective and Proactive Clusters were found to be significantly higher in Pre-encounter attitudes of racial identity than the African-American males in the Adaptive Cluster ($F = 4.60$, $p < .01$). Proactive and Adaptive males report higher levels of kinship social support than their Protective counterparts ($F = 3.30$, $p < .004$). Finally, males from the Protective Cluster were higher than males from the Adaptive cluster in calamity fears or in worries that some physical harm may befall them (Means $= 18.3$ vs. 14.5; $p < .05$).

Sample 2

ANOVAs for differences between the clusters revealed that all three clusters differed on each SORS-A factor (SRC: $F = 13.5$, $p < .0001$; CPR: $F = 44.8$, $p < .0001$; EFC: $F = 48.8$. $p < .0001$; RAT: $F = 3.34$, $p < .05$). Several interesting findings with respect to emotional adjustment and racial socialization orientation are reported here. The Proactive males appeared to be more socially introverted than the counterparts from the Protective and Adaptive clusters, respectively ($F = 3.13$, $p < .05$). The Proactive males demonstrated higher scores on the low self-esteem subscale than either Protective or Adaptive males ($F = 2.80$, $p < .05$). But, confirming of the adaptive resilience hypothesis, the Protective males showed higher levels of pessimism and learned helplessness than their counterparts from the Proactive and Adaptive clusters (Pessimism: $F = 2.71$, $p < .05$; Learned Helplessness: $F = 4.6$, $p < .02$). With respect to anger suppression, Proactive males showed higher levels compared to the other two clusters ($F = 2.60$, $p < .05$).

Sample 3

ANOVAs between the clusters revealed that all three clusters differed across each SORS-A factor (SRC: $F = 17.2$, $p < .0001$; CPR: $F = 33.4$, $p < .0001$; EFC: $F = 57.5$. $p < .0001$; RAT: $F = 27.9$, $p < .0001$). Significant differences on psychosocial variables between the three clusters were also identified. Some demographic variables were found to differ across the three clusters. With respect to a composite measure including orientation to spirituality, church attendance, and family religious conversation, Proactive males were significantly more spiritually involved and active than Protective males ($F = 2.97$, $p < .05$) with Adaptive males falling in the middle. One interesting finding that differentiated the three clusters was the number of persons living in the home ($F = 3.04$, $p < .05$). This finding approached but did not reach significance in Sample 2 but the trend was the same. The Protective males reported a significantly higher number of persons living in their home (Mean = 6.6 persons, sd. = 4.4) than either the Proactive (Mean = 4.7, sd = 1.9) and Adaptive males (Mean = 4.9, sd. = 1.7). Significant differences were found between the Protective and Proactive clusters.

Confirming the adaptive resilience hypothesis, it was found that compared to the Protective Cluster ($M = 34.5$; $SD = 6.6$), the adolescent men from the Adaptive ($M = 39.6$; $SD = 6.3$) and Proactive clusters ($M = 38.5$; $SD = 5.6$) showed significantly higher levels of kinship social support ($F = 3.1$, $p < .05$). This finding is consistent with the Sample 1 results. With respect to situational anger, teenage men from the Protective cluster ($M = 23.3$; $SD = 9.3$) reported significantly more anger than the young men from the Proactive ($M = 14.3$; $SD = 6.9$) and Adaptive clusters ($M = 14.9$; $SD = 6.8$; Overall $F = 6.6$, $p < .003$).

By analyzing whether the frequency of racial socialization communication (e.g., TERS) varies across the three clusters, we are able to bring some criterion validity to the cluster identities. It was found that young men from the Adaptive (M = 95.1; SD = 11.4) and Proactive Clusters (M = 94.9; SD = 11.2) reported a greater frequency of overall expressed multidimensional racial socialization messages than the Protective group (M = 81.5; SD = 12.1; F = 6.3, p < .003). That is, Proactive and Adaptive young men experienced more racial socialization than the Protective young men. Further analyses of the subscales of the TERS revealed that the Proactive and Adaptive males reported receiving significantly more spiritual coping socialization communication (F = 8.82, p < .004), more pride development socialization communication (F = 2.82, p < .05), and more racism struggles communication (F = 4.57, p < .01) than Protective males. No differences were found for cultural survival socialization. On the question of family conversation about racism, the Adaptive group, as expected, showed a significantly higher amount of conversation than the Proactive or Protective groups (F = 2.97; p < .05).

Combined Samples 1-3

ANOVAs between the clusters for each SORS-A factor revealed that all three clusters differed (SRC: F = 32.2, p < .0001; CPR: F = 57.7, p < .0001; EFC: F = 116.3, p < .0001; RAT: F = 154.4, p < .0001). Significant differences on psychosocial variables between the three clusters were identified.

There are two major sets of findings in this combined data set that corroborate previous findings. One relates to religiosity and the other to anger expression. First, the Proactive male group showed higher scores with respect to the religiosity questions compared to the Adaptive and Protective males groups, respectively (F = 1.60, p < .05).

Long-term reactive anger, anger control, anger suppression, and an overall greater frequency to express anger in any form were the five anger expression variables found to be significantly different among the three clusters. First, Adaptive males were found to be significantly higher in long-term reactive anger than Protective males (F = 2.61, p < . 05), in anger suppression than Protective males (F = 3.5, p < .05), and in overall frequency of anger expression than Proactive males (F = 3.6, p < .03). This represents the first bit of information that contradicts the adaptive resilience hypothesis. One last finding reveals that Proactive males show higher levels of anger control than either Adaptive or Protective males ($F = 4.9$, $p < .008$).

DISCUSSION

To what degree does African-American manhood psychological development depend upon the quality and extent of the cultural socialization of his family, peers, and society? It would be a strange experience to try and understand an African-American male teenager's psychosocial adjustment without some insightful knowledge about the messages and interactions that have contributed to his view of the world. This study is an initial step towards consolidating a theory of racial socialization identity perspectives for African-American males. A theory of racial socialization belief orientation is plausible and appears to consist of three distinct identity orientations.

Overall, most of the teenagers in all three samples tended to fall within the proactive cluster, followed by adaptive and protective clusters. It is suggested that all of the identity clusters hold a "both-and" quality to their character and definition. That is to say that there is something both resilient and risky for males from each group. It has been proposed that compared to either Proactive or Protective cluster profiles, the Adaptive racial socialization belief orientation will provide the healthiest psychosocial outcomes. This is an orientation to the world that recognizes the racial hostility that pervades, identifies that hostility and then keeps it at bay long enough to create a space for creative self-expression. These results have supported this hypothesis to a significant degree. For most psychosocial variables across all three samples, young teenage African-American males with the adaptive orientation were found to demonstrate positive adjustment.

Protective Racial Socialization Identity Orientation. In this study, Protective males showed lower levels of religiosity, a tendency to fear calamity, higher scores on measures of pessimism and learned helplessness, lower levels of kinship social support, more situational anger experience, less anger control, less conversation about race matters, and a greater number of persons living in their household compared to other identity orientations. On the positive side, Protective males showed lower levels of reactive anger experience and anger suppression and demonstrated an aversion to anti-African-American racial identity attitudes.

The protective identity orientation allows young men to act out on their anger in ways that can be risky and cathartic. This group of teenagers may represent a crew who are engaged in rebellious types of activities, who are quite aware of the racial hostility that surrounds them, and are quite adept at discerning the sincerity of others. The protective teen may see less hope in the world and in the worth of conventional behavior to effect meaningful success. He may have accepted that his efforts, no matter how creative or determined, will not result in positive outcomes; he may have personal or family experiences to support this outlook. This individual may be prone to less family influence and communication and may be less able to engage with family members primarily because of the less available psychological and possibly, physical space. This individual may have more experience with the streets and urban life and may have more intimate knowledge of the dangers that are intelligently avoided (Anderson, 1990). In a study on the psychological and ecological context of urban youth, those students who feared calamity the most were less likely to express anger openly and be more "streetwise" (Stevenson, in press-a). Long-term follow-up of Protective Black males would be interesting to understand more qualitatively their life experiences and their interactions with family, friends, and strangers. Such an analysis would lend more credence to this typology and determine the diversity within clusters that may go unnoticed in quantitative analyses.

Proactive Racial Socialization Identity Orientation. Males who adopt this orientation to the world appear to view the world through a spiritual orientation and may problem solve according to this orientation. The health and interpersonal benefits of a spiritual psychological orientation for Black adolescents are well-known (Benson & Donohue, 1990). Stevenson, Herrero-Taylor et al. (in press) have demonstrated that experiencing strong messages about how spirituality and religious appreciation are significantly related to decreased anger acting out and increased anger control. The proactive teens may make up what Elijah Anderson (1990) calls the "decent" student or Ogbu's (1985) "Ivy-Leaguer," who for the most part are raised to appreciate family and community and disdain outward aggression or disagreement. A tendency towards social introversion and low self-esteem are outcomes not incompatible with this orientation since living in the inner city may actually be or be perceived to be a dangerous, threatening world. Yet, it is a world the proactive teen may know of, but from a distance or vicariously through friendships, neighbors, and neighborhood happenings. Jarrett (1995) provides in-depth qualitative analyses of the complexity of experiences that families must apply to make sense of a confused world for their children. The family and church may be the place where most communication and interaction takes place, leaving contact outside of the world relatively minimal. Similarly, the family or the church may be the sole interpreter of the world beyond the front door, giving the teenager an owl's eye perspective on how to behave and how to understand and make sense of racial hostility and cultural pride. The fact that Proactive males reported higher levels of low self-esteem is worth investigating further. Perhaps this finding reveals the impact of a Black male who sees the harshness and limitations of one's social and racial status in the world while simultaneously being aware of his potential to rise above it. For teenagers, this dose of reality may be debilitating to one's self-esteem. As "decent" behavior goes, it is proposed that the Proactive male may ascribe to the same values of conventionality that are required in the school classroom and may do well academically.

Adaptive Racial Socialization Orientation. For the most part, those males with an adaptive orientation demonstrated psychologically healthy outcomes. Perhaps an adaptive orientation reveals a significant amount of time spent by caregivers in shaping this individual's worldview and character. The exceptions to the positive outcome findings may be some of the results in Sample 1 that showed that adaptive teenagers had higher levels of guilt and instrumental helplessness. Guilt may be a manifestation of responsibility and concern for others while instrumental helplessness may reflect an over-reliance upon others (e.g., family) for decision making. More research is necessary.

Overall, the adaptive teenager is one who tends to hold strong feelings about the world and can process both empowerment and oppression, hope and despair, victory and defeat. Because he can view the world with his eyes wide open, he sees both its hypocrisy and possibility. The African-American male who has this type of vision cannot help but develop and nurture a long-term type of anger, one that is very aware of the social injustices, societal inconsistencies, and the denied personal efficacy that is a derivative of these experiences (Chestang, 1972; Spencer, Swanson, & Cunningham, 1991). While the expression of this anger may be frequent and in a variety of ways, the adaptive male has the potential to translate this same energy into positive outcomes (Gibbs, 1994). Despite the awareness of a complex life reality, the adaptive teen has a moderate degree of anger control and feels a sense of hope about the world.

What does this research have to say about manhood development? One implication is that young African-American males respond to external influences in many different ways. It appears that for all three subgroups, the particular coping skills used to manage the complexity of life may be equally risky. Risk and resilience are not only resident within the same individual given the negative connotations attributed to Black male status in this country, but risk and resilience may be evident in the same coping strategy. To be aware of racism and to reject it may be an important psychological strategy in order to avoid self-denigration. Yet, having to reject racism and projected Black male fear by generating significant anger may be placing one in the center of controversy and also at risk for societal control. Anderson (1990) writes about the dilemmas of Black males who are in a "cultural catch-22" to protect their manhood through means that are self-destructive.

Another interesting direction derived from this research is the potential role of intrinsic and extrinsic religiosity and spirituality in promoting the psychological health of African-American youth. Several studies have identified this preventative potential with regard to HIV/AIDS at-risk behaviors and attitudes (Mays, 1989; Rupp & Stevenson, in press), and smoking, alcohol and drug abuse (Benson & Donahue, 1989). Benson and Donohue (1989) found that the more religious the teens were the less likely they were to engage in at-risk behaviors. Religiosity and collaboration with religious institutions must not be ignored as we assemble comprehensive intervention and research strategies for Black youth as within many religious contexts, the development of a social network of support systems is implicit (Stevenson, 1990).

This research may represent a slight alternative to the stage-based racial identity models. Perhaps the Nigrescence stage theory and the racial socialization theory of identity may be blended to account for subgroups across the racial identity spectrum from Pre-encounter to internalization. A student who advocates Pre-encounter attitudes but who was socialized to be proactive (e.g., focus on SRC, EFC, & CPR) may be significantly different in interpersonal style and problem solving than an African-American male who was socialized to be adaptive.

The need for replicating these three identity profiles remains. The limitations to this work rest on the selectivity of the sample–urban African-American males. Some concern may be raised regarding the small sample size in some clusters, except that the consistency of cluster identities across samples counters this argument. This research broadens the capacity to understand diversity among African-American teenage men and to propose specific intervention strategies that can be most effective for a particular subgroup. There are significant implications of this research for family and individual psychotherapy and parent education. Psychotherapists might benefit individuals and families of color by helping them to identify the types and amount of racial socialization messages given to their young men. Then, therapy can teach parents to balance the proactive and protective messages they give, knowing that such a stance may contribute to developing young men who are healthy and aware, thus increasing their options in evaluating societal inconsistencies and injustice. To warn Black youth about racial hostility without simultaneously celebrating their creative talent is most likely to result in a distorted and pessimistic view of self and the world. This is not to say that Proactive males are naively optimistic, but functionally optimistic. Perhaps Proactive males are more able to identify their strengths or able to rise above hostile circumstances (e.g., spiritual orientation). Adaptive racial socialization strategies can enhance young men's belief in a world obviously confused about race relations. It allows the individual to self-develop despite the obstacles facing him. Future research should also concentrate upon identifying similar identity profiles in young teenage women. The gender differences identified, if any, can help us add to our understanding of African-American manhood development. Finally, research must begin to investigate whether these identity profiles remain over time and whether environmental contexts erode or enhance the positive outcomes that are gained by maintaining an adaptive racially socialized identity.

REFERENCES

Anderson, E. (1990). *Streetwise*. Chicago: University of Chicago Press.

Benson, P. L., Donahue, M. J., & Erickson, J. A. (1989). Adolescence and religion: A review of the literature from 1970 to 1986. *Research in Social Scientific Study of Religion, 1*, 153-181.

Berndt, D. J. (1986). Multiscore depression inventory (MDI) manual. Los Angeles: Western Psychological Services.

Bowman, P., & Howard, C. (1985). Race related socialization, motivation, and academic achievement: A study of Black youths in three-generation families. *Journal of American Academy of Child Psychiatry, 24*, 134-141.

Boykin, A. W. & Ellison, C. M. (1995). The multiple ecologies of Black youth socialization: An Afrographic analysis. In R. L. Taylor (Ed.), *African American Youth: Their social and economic status in the United States*. Westport, CT: Praeger.

Boykin, A. W. & Toms, F. D. (1985). Black child socialization: A conceptual framework. In H. P. McAdoo, & J. L. McAdoo (Eds.), *Black children: Social, Educational, and Parental Environments*. Newbury Park: Sage.

Brofenbrenner, U. (1989). Ecological systems theory. *Annals of Child Development, 6*, 187-249.

Burke, P. J. (1980). The self: Measurement requirements from an interactionist perspective. *Social Psychology Quarterly, 43*, 18-29.

Cauce, A. M. & Gonzales, N. A. (1993). Slouching towards culturally competent research: Adolescents and families of color in context. *Focus: Psychological study of ethnic minority issues, 7*, 8-9.

Cross, W. E., Parham, T. A., & Helms, J. E. (1991). The stages of Black identity development: Nigrescence Models. In R. Jones (Ed.), *Black Psychology* 3rd Edition, (pp. 319-338). Hampton, VA: Cobb & Henry.

Gibbs, J. R. (1988). *Young, Black and male in America: An endangered species*. Dover, MA: Auburn House.

Gibbs, J. R. (1994). Anger in young Black males: Victims or victimizers? In R. G. Majors & J. U. Gordon (Eds.), *The American Black male: His present status and his future* (pp. 127-144). Chicago: Nelson/Hall.

Jarrett, R. L. (1995). Growing up poor: The family experiences of socially mobile youth in low-income African-American neighborhoods. *Journal of Adolescent Research, 10,* 111-135.

Johnson, E. H. (1989). The role of the experience and expression of anger and anxiety in elevated blood pressure among Black and White adolescents. *Journal of the National Medical Association, 81,* 573-584.

Johnson, E. H. (1990). Interrelationships between psychological factors, overweight, and blood pressure in adolescents. *Journal of Adolescent Health Care, 11,* 310-318.

Johnson, E. H. & Greene, A. (1991). The relationship between suppressed anger and psychosocial distress in African American male adolescents. *The Journal of Black Psychology, 18,* 47-65.

Jones, M. B., Peacock, M. K., & Christopher, J. (1992). Self-reported anger in Black high school adolescents. *Journal of Adolescent Health, 13,* 461-465.

Kaminoff, R. D. & Proshansky, H. M. (1982). Stress as a consequence of the urban physical environment. In L. Goldberger & S. Breznitz (Eds.), *Handbook of Stress: Theoretical and Clinical Aspects* (pp. 380-409). New York: Free Press.

Lal, B. B. (1995). Symbolic interaction theories. *American Behavioral Scientist, 38,* 421-441.

Majors, R. & Billson, J. M. (1992). *Cool pose: The dilemmas of Black manhood in America.* New York: Lexington Books.

Majors, R. G. & Majors, J. U. (1994). *The American Black male: His present status and his future.* Chicago: Nelson-Hall Publishers.

Marshall, S. (1995). Ethnic socialization of African American children: Implications for parenting, identity development, and academic achievement. *Journal of Youth & Adolescence, 24,* 377-396.

Mead, G. H. (1956). Play, the game, and the generalized other. In A. Strauss (Ed.), *The Social Psychology of George Herbert Mead.* Chicago: University of Chicago Press.

Njeri, I. (1993). Sushi and grits: Ethnic identity and conflict in a newly multicultural America. In G. Early (Ed.), *Lure and Loathing,* pp. 13-40. New York: Penguin Books.

Ogbu, J. (1985). A cultural ecology of competence among inner-city Blacks. In M. Spencer, G. Brookins, W. Allen (Eds.), *Beginnings: The Social and Affective Development of Black Children* (pp. 45-66). Hillsdale, NJ: Erlbaum.

Oyserman, D., Gant, L., & Ager, J. (1995). A socially contextualized model of African American identity: Possible selves and school persistence. *Journal of Personality and Social Psychology, 69.*

Pearlin, L. I. (1982). The social contexts of stress. In L. Goldberger & S. Breznitz (Eds.), *Handbook of Stress: Theoretical and Clinical Aspects* (pp. 367-379). New York: Free Press.

Peters, M. F. (1985). Racial socialization of young Black children. In H. P. McAdoo, & J. L. McAdoo, (Eds.) *Black children: Social, Educational, and Parental Environments.* Newbury Park: Sage.

Peterson, A. C. & Spiga, R. (1982). Adolescence and stress. In L. Goldberger & S.

Breznitz (Eds.), *Handbook of Stress: Theoretical and Clinical Aspects* (pp. 515-528). New York: Free Press.

Rupp, H. & Stevenson, H. C. (in press). Relevant measurement of HIV/AIDS prevention beliefs for African American youth. In D. C. Uneh (Ed.), Cross-Cultural Perspectives on HIV/AIDS Education, 18 pp.

Spencer, M. B. (1990). Parental values transmission: Implications for the development of African-American children. In J. B. Stewart & Cheatham (Eds.), *Interdisciplinary Perspectives on Black Families.* Atlanta: Transactions.

Spencer, M. B. (1995). Old issues and new theorizing about African-American youth: A phenomenological variant of ecological systems theory. In R. L. Raylor (Ed.), *Black youth: Perspectives on their status in the United States.* Westport, CT: Praeger (pp. 37-70).

Spencer, M. B., Swanson, D. P., & Cunningham, M. (1991). Ethnicity, ethnic identity, and competence formation: Adolescent transition and cultural transformation. *Journal of Negro Education,* 60, 366-387.

Spielberger, C. D. (1988). *State-trait anger expression inventory.* Odessa, Florida: Psychological Assessment Resources.

Stevenson, H. C. (1990). The role of the African-American church in the education of teenage pregnancy. *Counseling and Values, 34,* 2, 130-133.

Stevenson, H. C. (1992). Invisibility revisited: Challenging the negative images of black males. *AFTA Newsletter,* American Family Therapy Association, *42,* 15-19.

Stevenson, H. C. (1994a). Racial socialization in African American families: Balancing intolerance and survival. *The Family Journal: Counseling and Therapy for Couples and Families, 2,* 190-198.

Stevenson, H. C. (1994b). Validation of the scale of racial socialization for African American adolescents: Steps toward multidimensionality. *Journal of Black Psychology, 20,* 4, 445-468.

Stevenson, H. C. (1995b). Relationship of adolescent perceptions of racial socialization to racial identity. *Journal of Black Psychology, 21,* 1, 49-70.

Stevenson, H. C. (In press-a). "Missed, Dissed, & Pissed": Making meaning of neighborhood risk, fear and anger management in Black Youth. *Cultural Diversity and Mental Health.*

Stevenson, H. C. (In press-b). Theoretical considerations in measuring racial identity and socialization: Extending the self further. In R. Jones (Ed.), *Theoretical Advances in African American Psychology.* Hampton, VA: Cobb & Henry.

Stevenson, H. C. & Abdul-Kabir, S. (1996). *Reflections of hope from the "Bottom": Cultural strengths and coping of low-income African American mothers.* Proceedings of the Roundtable on Cross-Cultural Psychotherapy, Teachers College, Columbia University, New York.

Stevenson, H. C., Cameron, R., & Herrero-Taylor, T. (In press). Merging the ideal and the real: Relationship of racial socialization beliefs and experiences for African American youth. In D. Johnson (Ed.), *Racial Socialization Research,* Series in Advances in African American Psychology (R. Jones, Series Editor). Hampton, VA: Cobb & Henry.

Stevenson, H. C., Herrero-Taylor, T., & Cameron, R. (In press). Buffer zone: Impact of racial socialization experiences on anger expression in African American adolescents. In D. Johnson (Ed.), *Racial Socialization Research*, Series in Advances in African American Psychology (R. Jones, Series Editor). Hampton, VA: Cobb & Henry.

Stevenson, H.C., Reed, J., Bodison, P., & Bishop, A. (In press). Racism stress management: Racial socialization beliefs and the experience of depression and anger in African American youth. *Youth and Society.*

Promoting Critical Consciousness in Young, African-American Men

Roderick J. Watts

DePaul University

Jaleel K. Abdul-Adil

University of Illinois at Chicago

SUMMARY. In the U.S. as young African-American men in urban areas mature, they face oppressive social forces as well as the normative developmental challenges of adolescence. Nonetheless, much of psychology focuses on personal rather than sociopolitical development. As a basis for interventions aimed at sociopolitical awareness and action, this article presents a theory of oppression and sociopolitical development based on the work of Serrano García, Freire and others. According to this theory, critical consciousness (i.e., critical awareness about one's political, social and cultural condition) is an essential skill for sociopolitical development. This article also describes the "Young Warriors" program for building critical consciousness in high school aged young men. The results of this action-research project suggest that critical consciousness can be enhanced through a brief, eight-session intervention with the aid of Rap video, film and other products of mass culture. *[Article copies available for a fee from The Haworth Document Delivery Service: 1-800-342-9678. E-mail address: getinfo@haworth.com]*

INTRODUCTION

In this article, we describe an action-research project to promote critical consciousness and sociopolitical development in young,

---

[Haworth co-indexing entry note]: "Promoting Critical Consciousness in Young, African-American Men." Watts, Roderick J., and Jaleel K. Abdul-Adil. Co-published simultaneously in *Journal of Prevention & Intervention in the Community* (The Haworth Press, Inc.) Vol. 16, No. 1/2, 1997, pp. 63-86; and: *Manhood Development in Urban African-American Communities* (ed: Roderick J. Watts, and Robert J. Jagers) The Haworth Press, Inc., 1997, pp. 63-86. Single or multiple copies of this article are available for a fee from The Haworth Document Delivery Service [1-800-342-9678, 9:00 a.m. - 5:00 p.m. (EST). E-mail address: getinfo@haworth.com].

63

African-American men. Sociopolitical development is seen as an important step in combating oppression and promoting social, political and cultural liberation. The theory we describe in this article defines oppression as the unjust use of power to maintain social inequity. There can be little doubt that racial and gender inequity are a feature of US society. According to the Sentencing Project (The Sentencing Project, 1995) nearly one in three Black men in his twenties is incarcerated or on supervision. This rate is far higher than comparable figures for White men (1 in 15) or Hispanic men (1 in 8). For the last several years, there have been more young Black men incarcerated than in college. If African-American men manage to avoid prison, they face other perils: They have rates of homicide, substance abuse, unemployment, and inferior education unequaled by any other racial or gender group in this country (Staples, 1987). Life expectancy for Black men in Harlem is lower than that of men in Bangladesh (McCord & Freeman, 1990). According to some, Black men are now an "endangered species" (Gibbs, 1988).

For healthy development under these conditions, young men must develop sociopolitically as well as personally. Conventional interventions on coping, stress-management, conflict-resolution, and similar personal skill-building are necessary but not sufficient. An exclusive focus on individual psychosocial development neglects collective consciousness and action against social injustice. Sociopolitical development is a neglected area in youth development, so we highlighted it in this article. Nonetheless, in the field, our work attends to personal as well as community skills and views them as two sides of the same human-development coin. To understand the specific focus of this study of critical consciousness it is necessary to place it in a larger theoretical context–that of sociopolitical development. The presumption is that social injustice and inequity are outcomes of oppression, and that sociopolitical development helps oppressed people to recognize unjust social processes and acquire skills for social change. These new skills are part of *liberation behavior*–the action counterpart of the psychological changes associated with critical consciousness and sociopolitical development.

To understand the role of critical consciousness in sociopolitical development, it is necessary to return to the definition of oppression. The definition we use, based on the work of Moss (1991), Blauner (1972), and Serrano-García and Lopez Sanchez, (1992) has process and outcome components. As a process, it is the unjust exercise of power and the control over coveted resources in a way that produces and sustains social inequity. This inequity is a social consequence of *Asymmetry*–the unequal distribution of coveted resources among politically salient populations. In the case of race, this can be seen in the disparity between Blacks and Whites in health and wealth. Viewed as an outcome of these processes, oppression is the circumstances that result from long-term, consistent, and successful denial of resources. Critical consciousness is the ability to perceive this disparity and ask *why* it exists. As sociopolitical development continues, the person develops a social, political, and cultural understanding of the asymmetry.

An example of racial asymmetry in education funding was documented by Fairchild (1984). His statistical analysis of per-pupil expenditures found racial inequities in the Los Angeles school system. Similarly, Squires (1993) testified about his research on "redlining," the continuing racist insurance policies that undermine Black residential and business communities. Both of these are examples of oppression as *process*. On the outcome side, you see large classroom sizes, inadequate educational materials and children who ultimately receive a substandard education. Inadequate education and discrimination are two strikes against these young adults when they seek employment or further education. Poverty, joblessness, and even crime are predictable outcomes when this process of oppression is sustained over long periods.

Distinguishing between process and outcome is helpful for distinguishing outcomes such as multi-generational poverty, family disruption, drug abuse, anti-social behavior and violence from the processes that produce them. Mental health professionals may see the psychological outcomes as psychopathology, but they can also be viewed as adaptive strategies that evolved in response to oppressive social processes. Viewing oppression as a process trains our attention on the *means* by which inequality is created and sustained. Martin Luther King (1958) appreciated the interplay of oppressive processes and outcomes. Among his observations, he argued, "There must be a rhythmic alteration between attacking the causes and healing the effects" (p. 224). King also described how a conceptual and explanatory structure that relies wholly on individual functioning can distort our understanding of human behavior:

> . . . environmental problems of delinquency are interpreted as evidence of racial criminality. Crises in Northern schools are interpreted as proofs that Negroes are inherently delinquent. The extremists do not recognize that these school problems are symptoms of urban dislocation rather than expressions of racial inferiority. Criminality and delinquency are not racial; poverty and ignorance breed crime whatever the racial group may be. (p. 194)

Racism is an especially effective form of oppression that defines population membership by appearance or culture. At its core, it is an ideology of superiority in a broad range of areas: cultural, moral, intellectual, genetic, and spiritual. This notion of superiority, known more broadly by some scholars as white supremacy (Welsing, 1991) becomes the rationale for the exercise of power over racial groups such as African-Americans.

The Young Warriors program was designed to raise social, political, and cultural consciousness in young African-American men. More specifically, the curriculum develops critical consciousness skills that help young men understand oppressive processes and outcomes. We have worked with a range of ages, but most participants are in high school. The program was adapted from Paulo Freire's (1975) educational practices for critical consciousness. Derived from his related notion of "conscientization" it is "the process whereby people achieve an illuminating awareness both of the socioeconomic and cultural circumstances that shape their lives and their capacity to transform that reality" (Freire, 1975; p. 800, emphasis added). Critical consciousness is critical thinking, applied to the societal realm. Although critical consciousness training is political, it is not a form of indoctrination. For example, if a young man concludes that asymmetry among populations in the US is due to factors other than oppression, the program staff do not define this as a "wrong" conclusion.

The program goals for men in Young Warriors are as follows:

- *Developing critical consciousness skills.* Developing critical consciousness and critical thinking to help youngsters reevaluate the disruptive, violent and counterproductive behavior that is often glamorized in television, movies, music, and peer culture.
- *Learning about manhood.* Through a critical analysis of masculinity in mass culture and society, increase their awareness of how African-American manhood is constructed in contemporary society. Critically evaluate the notion of "Warrior" in history and in contemporary society.
- *Developing cultural awareness.* Examples, ideas, and traditions from African and African-American culture are infused throughout the curriculum.
- *Increasing the understanding of (and participation in) community development and social change.* African-American history has a long and distinguished tradition of action for human rights. Understanding these traditions from a critical perspective and adapting them to their own community's circumstances is an important goal. This becomes a means for some to channel "warrior energy" into community development and social change.

These goals originate from a stage model of sociopolitical development we adapted from the work of Serrano-García and Lopez-Sanchez (1992), and Ander-Egg (1980). This working theory has not yet been empirically evaluated (for more details on the theory, see Watts & Abdul-Adil, in press). The theory has five stages:

1. *Acritical Stage:* Asymmetry is not subject to critical thought and the capacity of critical consciousness is limited. The person may see inequity as the natural way of the world; that is, it is a "just world" and those with low status deserve it because they are inferior. Internalized oppression (thoughts and feelings of inferiority) can help sustain feelings of powerlessness or inferiority.
2. *Adaptive Stage:* The person may acknowledge inequity, but the system maintaining it is seen as immutable. Predatory,

anti-social or accommodation strategies are employed to maintain a positive sense of self and to acquire social and material rewards. Critical consciousness does not contribute to an understanding of the long term sociopolitical consequences of adaptive behavior or its role in maintaining oppression.

3. *Pre-Critical Stage:* Complacency gives way to a critical awareness of, and concerns about asymmetry and inequality. The value of adaptation is questioned.

4. *Critical Stage:* Critical consciousness skills undergo their most rapid development and use. Motivation is highest for learning about asymmetry by the analysis of the social and historical roots of asymmetry, injustice, and oppression. Critical consciousness will lead some people to conclude that the *asymmetry is unjust,* and that social-change efforts are needed. The person uses Adaptive strategies less frequently.

5. *Liberation Stage:* The experience and awareness of oppression are salient. Involvement in social action and community development is tangible and frequent. Adaptive behavior is eschewed. Critical consciousness is an established component of self.

Cultivating a social-change orientation is a challenge for action researchers who intervene through programs. Historically, social change has been a child of mass movements–not programs. Movements are associated with political culture, while programs are often a part of mainstream institutions and funding streams. According to Heaney (1995):

> . . . Cooperation with mainstream educational institutions takes its toll on staff for whom the limited interests of their sponsors dictate priorities and moderate action. There is no free lunch and programs which thought that the residuals of public funding would sustain the "liberatory" aspects of their program find that the obligations they have incurred under government funding so occupy staff that there is little time, energy, or incentive left for critical teaching and transforming action.

With this in mind, Young Warriors used four strategies for institutionalizing critical consciousness: (1) Always attempt to train local staff so that there is no on-going dependence on our trainers; (2) view the training as leadership development–identifying and nurturing activists who in turn energize others; (3) create political culture: produce a cadre of young men who can support each other's sociopolitical development; and (4) provide a measure of free work that is not subject to outside financial control.

Critical Consciousness: Training and Measurement Methods

The first challenge for our action-research team was developing a training strategy for enhancing critical thinking on social, political, gender and cultural topics while holding the interest of young men. To accomplish this we relied on rap music videos, television shows, and film as the subject matter for the training and as a stimulus for discussion. There were a number of advantages to using this material: it validates an art form the young men valued but adults often despise (so, when adults value it they gain credibility); it is ecologically and culturally relevant to the young men's life experience; and it covered a very wide range of contemporary topics from many different vantage points. The second challenge was devising a method for evaluating any gains in critical thinking.

Table 1 highlights some of the main components of critical thinking in the education literature, and their links to critical consciousness and the Young Warriors program. The sociopolitical version of critical thinking we call critical consciousness is akin to Kretovics (1985) definition of critical literacy: ". . . providing students not merely with functional skills, but with the conceptual tools necessary to critique and engage society along with its inequalities and injustices. . . . tools necessary for engaging in active critique at all levels of everyday life . . . " (p. 51).

This view of education and literacy is Freireian (1990) at its core. Our version adds ideas from the long tradition of social action in the African-American community, and the unique, urban, oppressed, hyper-segregated ecology so often described by rap artists. We based our training method on ideas from the education literature, particularly theories and exercises related to critical thinking. All of the educational theorists cited in Table 1 argue that critical thinking is a key academic skill that resists easy direct measurement. For training purposes we simplified critical consciousness into five

TABLE 1. Key Elements of Critical Thinking, Critical Consciousness and the Young Warriors Program

Elements of Critical Thinking from the Literature	Elements of Young Warriors Critical Consciousness Training (presented in the form of typical questions)
Judge the credibility of sources (Ennis, 1993).	Who is responsible for the production of these videos and films?
Using more of the information available in a stimulus (Hudgins & Edelman, 1988).	What did you see (or otherwise perceive and experience)? Say what you saw and heard first.
Judge quality of argument; Identify conclusions, reasons, assumptions. Draw conclusions, when warranted (Ennis, 1993).	What does it MEAN (interpretation)? What is the person trying to say? What is s/he trying to do?
Develop and defend positions. (Ennis, 1993).	Why do you think that? (defense) Why do you think that is what it means? Support what you think with evidence.
". . . working in both critical thinking and moral development simultaneously may have a mutual positive effect" (p. 125, Pierce, Lemke, & Smith, 1988).	What do you think/feel (values, emotions, sentiments) about what you saw or heard? Is what you saw and heard good, bad, or neither?
Action: Transform the System (Smith & Alschuler, 1976).	What would you do to make it better?

areas: (1) Perception based on the stimulus; (2) Interpretation and meaning; (3) Defense of interpretations; (4) Feelings about the stimulus; and (5) Action strategies. Consistent with the work of Pierce, Lemke, and Smith (1988), and others (e.g., Hudgins and Edelman, 1988) small group discussions were the heart of Young Warriors. The trainers primarily used Rap videos and film excerpts followed by questions (based on the right column in Table 1) as the strategy for promoting critical consciousness. The content themes of the video presentations fell into four broad areas: African-American masculinity, gangsta lifestyles, male-female relations, and community action and development.

The research questions were as follows: (1) Do the principle elements of critical consciousness as defined in the Young Warriors program correspond with actual discourse produced by program participants?

What other themes emerge consistently? (2) Can a content analysis procedure be devised as a reliable and valid means of measuring critical consciousness in the action context of weekly program discussions and training? (3) Can the Young Warriors program enhance critical consciousness over an eight week, eight session time period?

METHODOLOGY

Participants. The participants in this action research were African-American freshman and sophomore high school students (n = 32; M age = 15.5) in an impoverished Midwestern urban school. The students were recruited by a youth counselor from the school as part of an emerging manhood group formed by the counselor a few months earlier. School officials had informally identified some of these young men as "management problems." Although the sample was not random, it represented the kind of young men that institutions route to ancillary services because school officials see them as "at risk." Because this was a cooperative endeavor between school counselors and the university-based research team, we sought to meet the needs of our school associates by keeping the group open to new members throughout the eight-session program. Consequently, the program may be described as a drop-in group with a core of consistent participants. The drop-in format, along with numerous shifts in the school schedule by administrators, produced wide variations in attendance. Seven young men attended at least four of the eight sessions, but another 25 dropped in for one to three sessions. Among those who did not attend at least four sessions, the average number of sessions attended was 1.5. Session size ranged from five to 12 (mean = 9.3).

Procedure and Analysis

The program ran for eight, 40 minute sessions in the school plus one closing field-trip session held at the university, and they were conducted by the first author and a program assistant. Almost all featured one or two brief video presentations followed by a discussion. The first author and an undergraduate senior conducted the sessions. Sessions were audiotaped with informed consent.

A professional typist transcribed the session audiotapes using a leading word-processor software package. The investigators then imported the text in electronic form to NUD•IST (Non-numerical Unstructured Data Indexing Searching and Theorizing) 3.0.5 Power Version qualitative data analysis computer software. The software permits the researcher to create categories and to associate response units in the transcript with one or more categories. These categories (called "nodes") were organized hierarchically in a tree-like structure. The first author created the initial classification tree by reviewing and coding all response units in the transcript. A response unit began when a person started talking, and ended when someone else began speaking (sentence fragments were ignored). A total of 1,040 response units were classified. Some units were associated with multiple (up to three) nodes.

The first author then worked with three graduate student research assistants to revise and adjust the initial coding categories. Despite modifications to the initial coding scheme, reliability among the judges when coding independently was still unsatisfactory (less than 70% simple agreement). This phase was followed by another round of revision to the classification tree with a different research assistant and the second author.

The final version of the classification tree is presented in Figure 1. It is the product of a deductive (a priori, top down) as well as an inductive (bottom up) analysis process. At the top is the "root" node (0) that is the set of all responses in the analysis. Level 1 nodes are the first level of data differentiation. Nodes directly below a given node are called "children" and the one directly above is the "parent." The family tree analogy is an accurate one. It is a reminder of the relationships among nodes above and below the one of interest. All the nodes below a given node (its "descendants") contain responses that judges decided to classify more specifically; nonetheless, they remain related to the parent node and the ancestors above them in a general way. For example, if one judge coded a critical consciousness response unit as "See and Mean" (121) under "Video" (12) and another judge coded it "Judgment" (123) they were in agreement at level 2 because both classified it implicitly as a critical consciousness response about a video presentation (12). However they disagreed at the Level 3 nodes (121 vs. 123).

Consequently, reliability calculations can yield partial agreements among judges, as in this instance, as well as perfect matches. If they had both coded the response Judgment (123), agreement for that response unit would be perfect.

We derived the deductive tree elements from by the questioning strategy used throughout the program: What did you see (perception)? What did it mean (interpretation)? Why do you think that (defense)? What do you think or feel about it (judgment)? What could you do (action)? These questions were represented by the level three categories under the Video (12) and nonvideo (11) nodes. Critical consciousness responses were divided into video and nonvideo categories at level 2 because some responses came in the course of general conversation, while others were in reaction to video presentations. The level three categories are: See and Mean, Inference, Judgment, Change-action and Questioning. Definition for these and all other categories in the analysis are presented in Table 2.

The inductive analysis was part of our effort to understand the naturally occurring structure of critical consciousness, as it was found in the data. This "bottom up" approach yielded a category called "Questioning" and two child nodes called "Systems Action" and "Personal Action."

The other four level-one categories were also developed inductively. The details are omitted in Figure 1, but we will describe them briefly. The visual arts (Video and TV) category included responses about celebrities and screen and music artists. Gender responses fell into two categories, one for men and the other for women. Each had a child node for sex roles, but the men's category also contained one for warrior terminology, which came up a number of times because it was a theme in the curriculum. The Staff Talk category covered all remarks by the trainers. Culture and Race, Manhood, Critical Consciousness-related responses and Racism issues were under this category. There were also Staff Talk categories for warrior themes or specific men mentioned by name (all classified under manhood). Paralleling the Change-Action category for students, there was a level three Community Change category for Staff Talk under the Critical-Consciousness node.

The initial classification scheme had separate categories for

FIGURE 1. Classification Tree: Themes from Transcription Analysis*

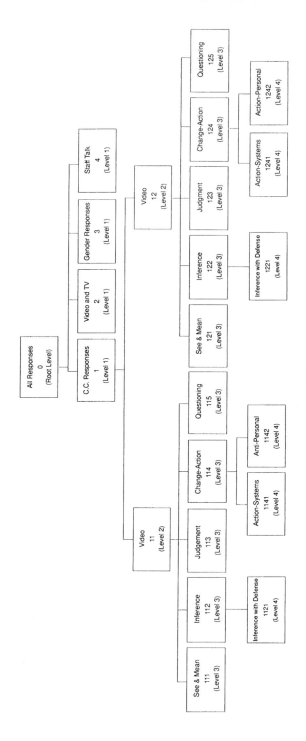

*The chart omits details of nodes that are unrelated to critical conscious (CC) categories.

"See" and "Mean" and no "Inference" category. In the final tree, See and Mean were collapsed into a single category, and Inference was added. The intent was to remedy the problem judges had in distinguishing response units with interpretive features from those which could be coded as purely perceptual ("See").

An interjudge agreement analysis was conducted to further evaluate the validity of the critical consciousness (CC) response units. Both authors and a research assistant independently classified all the response units using the categories in Figure 1. Judges classified each response unit into as many as three different nodes. The judges were instructed to classify each response unit as far down the tree (i.e., as specifically) as they could. This effort produced a four digit code (representing one node) for each classified response unit. Enough zeros were added to create a four digit code for response units classified at the more general, higher nodes (e.g., level 2 "Non-Video" codes were changed from 11 to 1100). Interjudge agreement was calculated through a combination of manual and computer analysis. As the earlier description of reliability suggested, agreement had to be evaluated at multiple levels.

Overall agreement was calculated as a percentage. The numerator was the number of agreements for CC codes among all three judges (the sum of all perfect and three-level agreements on the four-digit code) plus the number of perfect CC agreements (four-levels) among any two of the three judges. The denominator was the total number of response units coded as CC by at least one judge regardless of agreement. Because a response unit could have two, or even three agreements when permutations of two-judge agreement are included, percentages could exceed 100% for any one unit.

Overall agreement was 81%, with the breakdown by levels of agreement as follows: Three-judge perfect and partial (three level) agreement, 29%; three-judge nominal agreement (i.e., one and two level agreement) 18%; two-judge perfect agreement, 34%. To be conservative, partial and nominal two-judge agreement was not included in the calculation. These percentages are not independent, so it is not possible for each to reach 100%. Thus, only a sum of the various agreements is a good overall indicator of reliability. The expected level of agreement (i.e., the likelihood of chance agree-

TABLE 2. Critical Consciousness Category Definitions Used for Coding Transcripts

(abridged)

See and Mean
The person describes and articulates what he believed, perceived or experienced in response to something. The response emphasizes perception, rather than an abstract conclusion about what was perceived. Some interpretation is often involved, because sometimes perception doesn't tell you everything.

Inference
The difference between this and the see/mean category is a matter of degree. This node is the place for conclusions the respondent draws from his perceptions, that make very little specific reference to those perceptions. These are inferences about perceptions.

Defense
Did the person defend his point of view based on logic, values, or intuition/feeling to support his point? This category is for responses that include elements from a stimulus (video) or personal experience that defends the participant's point of view. Words like "because," or the use of if/then type logic phrases can clue you in that the respondent is defending his point of view based on logic, judgment, values, or feelings. Don't grade the quality, but it should make some sense as an explanation or reason for the respondent's view point.

Judgment and feeling
The person passes judgment on what he is talking about (limited to passing personal judgment on situations the respondent sees or hears in response to a stimulus). Scoring items "j" requires the presence of individual words that indicate approval/disapproval of what the respondent articulated. Typical words: like, hate, love (as in "I love..."), Good, bad, wrong, right, messed up, dope, straight, and similar slang terms indicating approval. Also code clearly insulting and harsh words or phrases: he was so stupid, he wasn't about nothin', etc.

Defense
For use with any inference category. A defense of the participant's point of view often includes or could include words like "because," or the use of if/then type logic phrases. These clue you in that the respondent is defending his point of view based on logic, judgment, values, or feelings. Don't grade the quality, but it should make some sense as an explanation or reason for the respondent's view point.

Change orientation
Many times these responses lack focus, but because this is a central point of interest of the research, it should be carefully coded. Any general or vague response that suggests the respondent sees a need for changes in individuals, social systems, institutions, society, or the world. More specific responses in this theme should be coded in the children of these nodes.

Action—Systems changes
Examples: this school needs to get some new teachers and a new attitude if we are going to learn anything before we graduate.

Action—personal
Action that could lead to some beneficial personal or social results. Examples: black people need to learn how to run businesses so they can get ahead. Black men need to stop hurting women because we need to work together to save our communities.

ment) is low given the large number of categories and multiple judgments per response unit.

RESULTS

Only the response units that judges agreed on in the ways described above were used to answer the research question "does the Young Warriors program enhance critical consciousness over time?" Figure 2 shows the number of CC responses per session as a percentage of all coded responses in each session. A second data series tracks the proportion of all coded responses by session, to show how the sheer volume of responses, of all types, increases over time. The results show a marked increase in the proportion of critical consciousness responses between session one and two and a second upward trend from session five until the final session (the final, wrap-up session emphasized the closure process rather than content).

Critical Consciousness in the Words of the Participants

Examining what students actually said is the best way to understand critical consciousness and the other coded categories. In this section we quote directly from the participants for each of the major categories. The following are some examples from the level three categories (see Figure 1). The most basic form of critical consciousness, See and Mean, included descriptive responses with very little abstraction:

> They talking about some of him and his friends—they were tripping; and he got up in the morning and went to see his girl, and he talks about his girl as a 'hoe,' then he started to go over to the shack to play some domino's with this 'hoe' and she . . .

The inference category differs from See and Mean because it can contain little descriptive information. Instead, it is a conclusion drawn from the stimulus. Inference suggests that the stimulus underwent additional cognitive processing. A simple inference can be just a reaction, an unsubstantiated opinion. For example, in response to a semi-autobiographical rap video, one student concluded: "He ended up learning life on his own." A more sophisti-

FIGURE 2. Proportion of Critical Thinking Responses by Session

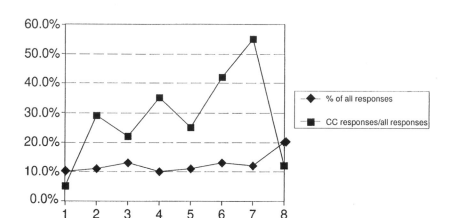

cated form of inference involves some substantiation. At this point, it includes another level 3 category, *Defense*. In the following response, the student links his perceptions and inference together to support his position: "The man with a badge on showing the role [of a police officer]. That's where I feel racial discrimination came in at." Note that the judges did not make a judgment as to the quality of the argument; the only thing necessary for coding was the linkage of an inference with an element of the stimulus. Despite this liberal coding rule for defense, it was observed infrequently.

Judgment responses showed evidence that the student tested the stimulus against his own values and verbalized approval or disapproval. The judge coded this example judgment and gender: "You shouldn't call a woman a female dog, she's not a female dog." Here are three other examples verbalized one after another by three students in response to a video stimulus:

"He was hanging out with the wrong crew."
"He didn't grow up in the right environment."
"He wasn't raised right in his family."

Unfortunately, fine-grained analyses for feeling were not reliable; only instances with clearly judgmental words like right and wrong, bad, and messed-up, produced reliable results. For example, when a student said "Yeah and how warriors stand by their women because your woman is supposed to stand by you," "I think she wants too much," . . ."She wants a lot of things that she can't get. She wants money" the judges did not reach consensus that it was an expression of personal values. It may be that voice inflection or context influenced the judges. They may have seen it as simply an inference from the stimulus. In any event, the coding definitions for this category never reached a satisfactory level of refinement.

Two examples from the Staff Talk category taken from different sections of the transcript reveals the coaching process that shaped or brought out critical consciousness in the youngsters:

> Let's talk about what's going on in the neighborhood if there are some things you can change in this neighborhood, what would you try to change? (pause) If you could change some things going on in this community, what would be some of the things you'd want to change? (coded Change-Action)

> Why do you think that is? Remember, I think I heard you say that's why they don't like us [black men] anyway, because we use them or something like that. Why do you think brothers hit sisters? (coded Gender)

The following is an uninterrupted exchange between the trainer and students prior to a video presentation in an early session (number 2) of the program. It illustrates poverty of response in early sessions and the coaching by the trainers:

Student: [is the name of the video] 'Street life'?
Trainer: Street life–how many people here have seen that? Okay.
   Can anybody tell me anything about the video?
Student: I only saw it a couple of times.
Trainer: Did you think about any thoughts or feelings about what was going on in the video when you saw it?
Student: Not really.
Trainer: Well good, then I have my work cut out for me. As I told you before, one of the purposes of this, instead of just watching videos for the beats and for 'the women,' as I believe someone

had said. . . I want you to look at it a little bit differently. I want you to pay attention to what is going on. So flip over this thing [handout]. See where it says Critical Consciousness at the top? That's the term we use to describe how you watch things. That means you watch things critically and you stay alert. So when you look at this video, I want you to pay attention to what you see and I also want you to think about the message.

In later sessions, students began to make the difficult transition from critique to creativity. They began to engage in constructive criticism in the form of suggestions or ideas that could improve a situation. Such responses were classified as *Change-Action*. The following in an unedited series of exchanges from session seven. Responses were more complex, and there was more evidence of critical consciousness:

> I don't think that's good because although we got our heads on straight, they looking towards some other people that might come up to them saying being in a gang is the right thing. I don't think that's a good idea. I think what it is is role models. We need role models in general. The little ones and big ones. I think that's what it is.

Trainer: You say sports is something that sometimes brings people together? Okay, that's one idea.

Student: That's a good idea too, because you know, say, like one group have a dispute with another group. You could battle it out on the court or something like that. You don't have to go out there and shoot nobody over disputes.

Student: Anything is possible. Anything can be talked over because it ain't nothing worth being killed over.

Trainer: We've got two good suggestions. We already got sports, pulling teams together, mixing up folks on trying to win a basketball game is one way to promote unity. Other ideas?

Student: Something you could do is keep your neighborhood clean.

Trainer: Keep your neighborhood clean. So that's one thing. In fact, when I was walking down the hall here, I saw a whole lot of trash in the halls. So you might not even have to go outside to do that. Okay, keeping things clean. What happens when people live in a clean environment?

Student: You feel much safer. People respect the neighborhood more.

Trainer: People respect the neighborhood more. Okay, and they respect themselves more too.

Student: White people pass our neighborhood and it's all dirty so they degrade it down to a lower level. If it's real clean, then they think lightly of it.

Trainer: Okay, so the way the neighborhood looks, the way the school looks, those are important things you could do. Other kinds of ideas you have that you can make something of the community?

Student: You could have seminars and talk about various ideas, activities, such as sports, going on trips, and stuff.

Trainer: So we have some things to do other than just kind of hanging out in the streets. You all came up with some good ideas.

DISCUSSION

The purpose of this research was to explore the construct of "critical consciousness" as it occurs in the discourse of high school students participating in a school-based intervention. The intervention, Young Warriors, was designed to elicit and develop critical thinking and critical consciousness skills, with the latter seen as a more specific, sociopolitical version of the former. According to the theory of sociopolitical development we presented, critical consciousness is a fundamental and necessary skill for understanding oppression. The first specific research question posed was: Do the principal elements of critical consciousness as defined in the Young Warriors program correspond with actual discourse produced by program participants? What other themes emerge consistently? The second, related research question was: Can a content analysis procedure be devised as a reliable and valid means of measuring critical consciousness in the action context of weekly program discussions and training?

The answer to both questions is a qualified yes, but there are a number of limitations to consider. Judges had great difficulty distinguishing the a priori categories of "Perceptions based on a stimulus" and "meaning." To remedy this problem, perception and meaning were combined in the second phase of analysis, and a new category "Inference" was added. Reliability improved considerably. There are at least two reasons why adding the inference category may have improved agreement. *Inference* is "The act or process of deriving logical conclusions from premises known or assumed to be true," whereas *meaning* is not explicit about a cognitive process: "something that is conveyed or signified; sense or significance" (American Heritage Dictionary, 1985). Apparently, judges could more reliably agree on the presence of a cognitive process. The second reason why Inference improved reliability may be that it better accounts for the role of perceptions as "premises" for the inferential process. Both of these reasons may have helped judges look for conclusions drawn from a set of perceptual premises, and distinguish them from simple see-and-mean responses.

This finding has practical as well as theoretical significance. It suggests that training should focus on the cognitive process that occurs between assumptions about the stimulus and conclusions drawn from it. Based on these findings, we have decided to add a new prompt to our coaching and training after a participant makes an unsupported inference: "Tell me how you got there!" In other words, what chain of thoughts, associations and feelings got you from what you saw, to what you think it meant. We will continue to use the term *meaning* in our work because it is simpler, but our approach to this element of critical consciousness had changed.

Although we made no explicit hypothesis about the specific components of critical thinking, we did expect to find some evidence of *Defense* of interpretations, but it occurred very infrequently. Moreover, responses classified as defense were not especially well developed. It may have been a problem of the intervention, because our coaching strategy was less developed in this area. To improve coaching in future programs, trainers will try the phrase "Tell me how you got there!" to help students pay more attention to the process of drawing a conclusion and the skills needed to verbalize it. Their explanation of the process will be, in effect, their defense.

The fourth element of critical thinking is judgment. This proved difficult to code reliably. In the end, judges were limited to a very simple, dichotomous definition of feeling–good or bad sentiments–expressed in very explicit terms. Values, sentiments, intuition and feeling are an important element of critical consciousness for men especially, because they are attributes outside the masculine stereotype. Unfortunately, we were unable to devise a refined and satisfactory way of coding it.

Lastly, there were Action Strategies. Constructive criticism–the transition from critique to creativity–is always more demanding than simply finding fault. Perhaps this is why there were few sophisticated suggestions for social and community action. Shortcomings in the program, due to its length and our coaching methods, may also have played a part. We did not stress this element until late in the program as we began to see more evidence that the other components of critical thinking were in place. In addition we had little confidence in the distinctions that we made between personal and systemic forms of action because there were so few coded. Interrelationships between self and society are complex matters that deserve more attention than was possible here.

There is more to be said about the second research question on the coding of group discussion. Above all, it is an extraordinarily time consuming and tedious process, even at the modest level of rigor employed in this study. There is, nonetheless, a payoff for action researchers. The conceptual clarity produced from our many spirited discussions of critical consciousness during the development of the definitions sharpened our training technique and reinforced our confidence in the program. For practitioners, however, it would be much more efficient to listen to transcripts and selectively record sophisticated or interesting responses. Staff would then discuss these highlights in meetings to build a common core of training techniques and objectives.

Future research must cope with a bewildering array of analytical and computational choices without the benefit of established conventions. We chose to process the data line by line, but in our future work we may attempt to analyze the text using discussion topics as the unit of analysis. For instance, all discussion on a single actor, or a single video, or a specific topic, would be processed as a unit. Although this complicates decisions about the boundary of each analytical unit, it would reduce the loss of data due to sentence fragments that make reference to prior statements. The final re-search question was less theoretical and more relevant to program evaluation: Does the Young Warriors program enhance critical con-sciousness over time? An answer to this question must be preceded by an acknowledgment of the shortcoming of the design by exper-imental standards. There was no comparison group and no within-subject design. At best, it was a within-group design where the group served as its own control in an eight-point time series analysis. However, because it was a drop-in group, any intervention effect was probably attenuated by the intermittent participants who did not re-ceive the same "dose" of training as those who attended regularly.

Yet, despite these limitations, the findings were encouraging. Over time, there was an increase in the proportion of critical think-ing responses. The proportion peaked in the seventh of eight ses-sions (the eighth session was a wrap-up). We concluded from this that one of two changes occurred among participants: Either their critical-thinking skills improved, or their willingness to demon-strate their existing critical thinking skills in the sessions increased. We suspect both happened. In any case, we counted this as a prom-ising finding because if students are unwilling to openly engage in intellectual discourse, they have no opportunity to practice and develop their cognitive and oral skills. One of the first tasks in our work was to develop a safe environment with supportive norms so that students would not fear ridicule or humiliation when taking intellectual risks. This required at least two or three sessions. Once students felt safe, they could begin taking risks and developing their skills.

In future practice, there are many steps remaining. One of the most important steps is to use a foundation in critical thinking to develop critical consciousness–critical thinking's sociopolitical counterpart. This is an evolutionary rather than revolutionary step that simply requires more political and cultural content in the cur-riculum. The training process itself changes little. Critical con-sciousness training can take on many different looks, ranging from a reform-minded version of school civics, to a subversive strategy for building revolutionary political culture. In whatever guise, the purpose of critical consciousness is to nurture social change agents.

This research did not demonstrate the place of critical consciousness in the larger process of sociopolitical development. Our future plans are to take critical consciousness out of the classroom and into action. Hands-on community awareness and development projects that enhance students' feelings of self-efficacy and empowerment are in order. Specifically, internships in community organizations, video production (e.g., community and biographical mini-documentaries), letter-writing campaigns, entrepreneurial activities and more strident forms of collective action. For those who wish to keep critical thinking more closely tied to academic work, there is a growing body of literature on media education (Masterman, 1993) that calls for teachers to educate youngsters on mass culture. There are also numerous ways of linking rap to poetry, English, literature appreciation, drama, and other art forms. We urge those who would use rap as a vehicle for youth development to be cautious, however. In unskilled hands, certain types of rap can serve to glamorize misogyny, materialism, gangsta lifestyles and the other sensationalized negative elements of hip-hop culture. This is especially true when adults lend it legitimacy by bringing it into the classroom. At its best, it meets young people where they are, and gives them a familiar place from which to explore new intellectual ground.

REFERENCES

Ander-Egg, E. (1980). Metodologíca y práctica del desarrollo de comunidad. Espana: UNIEUROP.

Blauner, R. (1972). *Racial oppression in America.* San Francisco: Harper & Row.

Ennis, D. (1993). A single multidimensional model for discrimination, identification and preferential choice. Special Issue: Tactile pattern recognition.

Fairchild, H. (1984). School size, per-pupil expenditures, and academic achievement. *Review of Public Data Use, 12,* 221-229.

Freire, P. (1975). Cultural action for freedom. *Harvard Educational Review Monograph, 1.*

Freire, P. (1990). Education for critical consciousness. NY: Continuum.

Gibbs, J. (1988). Conclusions and recommendations (pp. 339). In J. Gibbs (Ed.), *Young, Black and Male in America.* Dover, MA: Auburn House.

Heaney, T. (1995). Issues in Freirean Psychology. *Thresholds in Education (On line).* Available: http://nlu.nl.edu/ace/Resources/Documents/FreireIssues.html

Hudgins, B., & Edelman, S. (1988). Children's self-directed critical thinking. *Journal of Educational Research, 5,* 262-273.

King, M.L. (1958). *Stride toward freedom.* New York: Harper & Row.

Kretovics, J. (1985). Critical literacy: Challenging the assumptions of mainstream educational theory. *Journal of Education, 167* (2), 50-62.

Kvaraceus, W. (1965). *Negro self concept: Implications for school and citizenship.* New York: McGraw Hill.

Masterman, L. (1993). The media education revolution. *Canadian Journal of Educational Communication, 22,* 5-14.

McCord, C. & Freeman, H.P. (1990). Excess mortality in Harlem. *New England Journal of Medicine, 322,* 173-177.

Moss, J. (1991). Hurling oppression: Overcoming Anomie and self hatred. In B. Bowser (Ed.), *Black male adolescents: Parenting and education in community context.* Lanham, MD: University Press of America.

Pierce, W., Lemke, E., & Smith, R. (1988). Critical thinking and moral development in secondary students. *High School Journal, 71,* (3), 120-126.

Serrano-García, I., & Lopez-Sanchez, G. (August, 1992). *Asymmetry and oppression: Prerequisites of power relationships.* Presented at the annual convention of the American Psychological Association, Washington, DC.

Squires, G. (1993). Insurance redlining–still fact, not fiction. On-line article based on testimony presented to the House Subcommittee on Consumer Credit and Insurance, February 1993. Available at *NHI Shelterforce on-line:* http://www.nhi.org/online/ issues/79/isurred.html

Staples, R. (1987). Black male genocide: A final solution to the race problem in America. *Black Scholar.*

The Sentencing Project (1995). *Facts about prisons and prisoners: The growing corrections system.* Washington, DC: The Lindesmith Center.

Watts, R., & Abdul-Adil, J. (in press). Psychological aspects of oppression and sociopolitical development. In R. Newby & T. Manley (Eds.), *The poverty of inclusion, innovation and interventions: The dilemma of the African-American underclass.* Beacon Press.

Welsing, F.C. (1991). *The Isis papers: The keys to the colors.* Chicago: Third World Press.

The RAAMUS Academy:
Evaluation of an Edu-Cultural Intervention
for Young African-American Males

Kenneth L. Ghee
Jim Walker
Anna Cash Younger
University of Cincinnati

SUMMARY. The RAAMUS Academy (Responsible African-American Men United in Spirit) pilot project was initiated to provide a structured after-school learning environment for self development and academic achievement. It is based on "Edu-Culture" the process of using cultural identity as a catalyst for academic motivation. One hundred academy participants were administered a host of behavioral and attitudinal indices on cultural and academic related behaviors and attitudes (schools, sports, play, knowledge of Black history) using a new instrument, the SQAK (Student Questionnaire on Academic Performance, Cognitive Development and Social Knowledge). GPA, and self esteem were also assessed pre and post. Increases were found in knowledge of Black history, frequency of after school academic behavior and self esteem. Modest decreases were seen in social influence by others and social recreation. Parental feedback was highly positive and indicated a strong desire for after school programming for young men. The findings are discussed in the context of further development of the SQAK and future youth interventions. *[Article copies available for a fee from The Haworth Document Delivery Service: 1-800-342-9678. E-mail address: getinfo@haworth.com]*

[Haworth co-indexing entry note]: "The RAAMUS Academy: Evaluation of an Edu-Cultural Intervention for Young African-American Males." Ghee, Kenneth L., Jim Walker, and Anna Cash Younger Co-published simultaneously in *Journal of Prevention & Intervention in the Community* (The Haworth Press, Inc.) Vol. 16, No. 1/2, 1997, pp. 87-102; and: *Manhood Development in Urban African-American Communities* (ed: Roderick J. Watts, and Robert J. Jagers) The Haworth Press, Inc., 1997, pp. 87-102. Single or multiple copies of this article are available for a fee from The Haworth Document Delivery Service [1-800-342-9678, 9:00 a.m. - 5:00 p.m. (EST). E-mail address: getinfo@haworth.com].

87

STATUS OF AFRICAN-AMERICAN EDUCATION

Ideally, education is the vehicle through which knowledge, skills and values are transmitted. However, for African-Americans, the U.S. educational system continues to fail. For example in 1990, nearly half (44%) of African-Americans were illiterate, compared to 16% of European-Americans (U.S. Dept. Of Commerce, 1990). Several scholars have examined the source of this problem for African-Americans (Boykin, 1986; Hilliard, 1985; Reed, 1988). Shaped by racism, the social forces that tend to *motivate* European-Americans to achieve academically, instead *divert* African-Americans from educational pursuits, consequently weakening their intrinsic motivation to achieve. Alternative educational programs and institutions are needed to re-direct African-American students toward academic aspirations (Bell & McGraw-Burrell, 1988; Ghee, 1990; Hale-Benson, 1988). According to Ghee (1994), three primary *edu-cultural* (social, cultural and educational) deficits must be addressed to make alternative programs effective: (1) *Miseducation.* In the historical and cultural milieu of U.S. education, only students with European ancestry were considered consequential (Thorndike, 1939). In modern U.S. education, the contribution of African-Americans to society remains undervalued (Castinell & Pinar, 1993; Nobles, 1990). Influenced by miseducation, African-American students are deficient in their cultural knowledge which leads to diminished dignity, pride, and self-esteem (Akbar, 1984; Woodson, 1933); (2) *Mass Media Influence.* U.S. media promotes conformity to the dominant Eurocentric norms, values, practices, and institutions (Rhodes, 1995; Kellner, 1995). U.S. media fails to reflect the diversified African-American experience (Azibo, 1988; Hall, 1995). Further, the primary role for African-Americans is the situation comedy (Wilson & Gutierrez, 1993). Thus, African-Americans (especially adult males), are rarely portrayed with positive qualities, such as morality, intelligence, leadership, and cultural allegiance (Hall, 1995; Rhodes, 1995). Consequently, the mastery of intellectual, spiritual, and cultural interests are de-emphasized, while the mastery of athletic and entertainment skills are emphasized. In addition, there is national concern regarding the behavioral effects of the ubiquitous television themes of sex and violence (Korenzy-Felipe et al., 1990). Considering the recent saturation of *gangsta rap* music in the media, with its themes of violence, sex, drugs, defiance of authority, female denigration, and ethnic disunity (Hansen, 1995; Baker, 1989; Watts & Abdul-Adil,1994) concerns about exposure to this rap music genre seems justifiable. Johnson et al. (1995), found that viewers of rap music videos with violent content reported more acceptance of violence than viewers of nonviolent videos or control group members. Dotter (1987) found that music fans are likely to emulate the performing artists. Given the recent criminal charges and murders of popular African-American rap artists, these findings are extremely disturbing. Of particular concern is the impact of these events on African-American youth (Johnson, 1991), especially urban teenagers, since ninety-seven percent of them enjoy rap music and Hip-Hop culture (The MEE Report, 1995); (3) *Mainstream and African-American cultural paradigms conflict.* African-Americans share a common set of sociocultural realities that generally conflict with mainstream culture and its processes and methods of education (Boykin, 1986; Hale-Benson, 1988; Bell & McGraw-Burrell, 1988). According to Boykin (1986), a triple quandary exists for African-Americans which requires negotiation between mainstream, minority, and Black cultural experiences. Hilliard (1976) determined that the characteristics of U.S. schools were consistent with Euro-American cultural orientation, but were inconsistent with African-American cultural dimensions. Shade (1982) found cultural differences in learning styles, world view and social cognition.

Within the African-American culture, young male subculture has its own identity and rules (Ghee, 1990; Gibbs, 1988; Madhubuti, 1990). Moreover, within this subculture, there are additional overlapping influences, such as gangs, drugs and hip-hop (The MEE Report, 1995). These influences are so pervasive, that they compromise the achievement motivation of many African-American males. For example, in peer settings, young African-Americans are stigmatized, even punished for positive academic behaviors (e.g., reading, getting good grades) (Kunjufu,1988).

COUNTERING EDUCATIONAL DIVERSIONS:
AFRICAN-AMERICAN MALES

Community programs designed specifically to address the needs of the young African-American male subculture have proliferated over the past few years. Watts (1993) in his review of 40 manhood development organizations from 14 states discovered six central themes for youth empowerment: family; culture; race; community; behavior; psychosocial development; and spirituality. Consistent with these themes is the *RAAMUS Academy*, an after-school edu-cultural program, that redirects African-American male youth from the various educational diversions in the youth subculture while inspiring and educating young African-American males about cultural awareness and academic achievement (Ghee, 1990; Ghee 1994). RAAMUS is an acronym which stands for *R*esponsible *A*frican *A*merican *M*en *U*nited In *S*pirit. Two of the major evaluations outcomes expected in this two year pilot study of the RAAMUS Academy were: (1) Young African-American male students who participated in the RAAMUS Academy would demonstrate increased knowledge of African-American history and cultural identity from pre intervention to post intervention; (2) RAAMUS Academy participants would demonstrate increased scholastic motivation, and school performance from pre-intervention to post intervention.

METHOD

Participants. A total of 100 African-American male youth were recruited through a radio talk show, a community newsletter, African-American cultural events, and community organizations serving African-American families. The mean age of participants was 12.2 years of age with a range from 8 to 17. Eighty-five percent of parents filling out the parent survey were mothers and 15% fathers. Parent ages ranged from between 25 and 30 to between 41 and 45. The mean age range was between 36 and 40 (42% of the sample). Thirty-three percent were married, 32% divorced, 24% single and 12% listed other. Only 21% had less than or equal to high school education, with 43% having at least a college degree. The remaining 38% reported having some college credits but never graduating.

Twenty-four of the families included the two biological parents. Sixty percent were single parent families, 12% included one biological and one stepparent and 4% were classified as other. Seventy-six percent of mothers were working full time and 60% of the fathers were working full time. Family income ranged from less than $10,000 to over $55,000. The median income range was between 25 and 30 thousand dollars. Finally, family religion classification revealed that 52% were Baptist, 12% Protestant, 9% Catholic, 5% Muslim, 5% Methodist and 17% other.

Instruments. Parents were administered a 12 item demographic questionnaire which included sex, age, education, family composition, work status, family income and religion and a 15 item Parent Feedback Questionnaire (at the end). This questionnaire was developed for this study to assess parents' perceptions of the program and its impact on the attitudes and behavior of their sons.

The "Student Questionnaire on Academic Performance, Cognitive Development, and Social Knowledge" (SQAK) was developed for this study by the first author, based on a review of the limited literature and instrumentation relevant to the unique ecology of young, urban, African-American males (Ghee, 1994). The SQAK is a 125 item open ended and Likert type questionnaire which assesses youth academic and social attitudes and behaviors, future aspirations, African-American role models, and knowledge of Black history. Twenty-two items are open-ended or sentence completions, and the remaining 103 use a 4-point Likert scale. Sample questions from the SQAK are provided elsewhere (Ghee, 1994). Average completion time was 40 minutes. The senior author constructed five a priori conceptual domains based on common themes among items: perceived interests, perceived competence, perceived importance, frequency of behavior, and self esteem. Within these domains were four psychosocial areas of interest: academics (e.g., reading), sports (e.g., basketball), social recreation (e.g., computer games), and creativity (e.g., art).

Procedure. The goals of Academy workshops were to facilitate meaningful interpersonal exchange between students and staff mentors, to enhance student academic motivation, to teach African-

American history, to build high self-esteem, and to foster cultural identity. To accomplish these goals, the curriculum included extensive book, video, and audio libraries on African and African-American history and education. The RAAMUS Academy used ten curriculum activity modules for achieving the program objectives. Each module was implemented in thirty or sixty minute segments utilizing a variety of audio and video strategies as outlined above. The ten modules for maximizing stimulation, and cultural relevance are: affiliation; excitation; inspiration; education; self-exploration; indoctrination; association (brotherhood); acculturation; evaluation; and graduation. These modules are described in detail elsewhere (Ghee, 1994). The twelve three-hour sessions were distributed over eight weeks (i.e., two-month interventions). One after-school session from 6pm to 9pm was held each week and alternating Saturday sessions from 11am to 2pm. Two groups were run simultaneously with the first group meeting on Tuesdays and the second group on Wednesdays. Both groups came together for the alternating Saturday sessions. Parental consent was obtained before program participation. The program was partially funded by a small grant from the Ohio Board of Regent's Minority Urban Research Grants Program. Additional funds were supplied through a $50 student registration fee and donations by the research and program staff.

Use of auditory and visual stimuli. A significant percentage of counselor referrals for school age African-American children are for academic and behavioral problems, particularly hyperactivity and attention deficit disorder (Allen & Majidi-Ahi, 1989). Many of these behavior problems may be, in part, due to the relatively low sensory stimulation environment of traditional education. Thus, the RAAMUS Academy incorporated both visual and auditory stimulation. Most workshops were conducted with choreographed music, including jazz, African drumming, story telling, and rap. This format is consistent with the recommendations of many educators who suggest that methods for teaching that make learning more stimulating help renew academic interest and concentration (Wlodkowski, 1990). It is also consistent with more recent calls for the utilization of music, specifically the rap music genre, for reaching African-American youth (Watts & Abdul-Adil, 1994; Abdul-Adil, 1992; Hale-Benson, 1988). For example, the official Academy school song was written as a positive rap song in which students performed in various public forums.

The RAAMUS Academy also incorporated an array of visual stimuli in the physical environment as well as in workshop curricula. The physical environment was furnished with cultural artifacts, pictures, animation, art, and other visual images of the positive African-American experience. Many RAAMUS workshops used video documentaries, popular movies, as well as specially tailored video productions designed to stimulate discussion of social issues and cultural identity development. Supplementary visual and conceptual stimulation was provided by warrior art, graphic carvings, costumes, tee shirts, RAAMUS super hero comic books, posters, and the utilization of visual imagery. The curriculum also included parent involvement and parent-child interactive activities aimed at reinforcing program goals in the home. The Academy included a follow-up booster component comprised of weekly study sessions on a college campus and a parent Advisory Board.

The SQAK was administered in the beginning of the program and at the end. Parents were administered the demographic questionnaire at baseline, and after the program, parents completed the Parent Feedback Questionnaire. School GPA was obtained at baseline, three months after the program, and at one year follow up.

RESULTS

The SQAK. The investigators grouped the 103 Likert items on the SQAK into nineteen composite variables addressing each area of interest (i.e., academics, sports, social recreation, and creativity) within each domain (i.e., interests, competence, importance, frequency of behavior, and self esteem). Social recreation and creativity items were combined into a single domain since they seemed to elicit similar responses. Only items that correlated at least 0.40 with the sum of all the items in its respective composite variable were included in the final composite. Mean percentage time spent at after-school academic behaviors, sports behaviors, social behaviors, and creativity behaviors for the entire group were derived by adding up individual activities in each category and dividing by the sum total number of activities in order to obtain a percentage score for each individual. These percentages, per individual, were then averaged over the entire group in order to obtain group mean percentages for each after-school behavior category.

Attitudinal and Behavioral Changes from Pre to Post Intervention

The composites along with examples of the component items are presented in Table 1. T-tests, comparing pre and post intervention composite scores, and after school mean percentages, controlled for the test-wise error rate, are also presented in Table 1. Internal consistency reliablity coefficients (Cronbach's Alpha) ranged from .50 for Black History Knowledge to .70 for Creative Importance.

Among the school-related variables, a significant increase in the frequency of "after school academic behavior," was produced, which included the frequency of reading, writing, and doing homework ($t = 3.10$, $p < .01$). A second area related to cultural, as well as academic, development showed improvement as well. "Black history knowledge" showed a significant increase ($t = 5.28$, $p < .001$) indicating that students could spontaneously retrieve more Black history information after, than before, the program. This variable was derived by a numeric count of the number of references given in response to the question "Name at least 10 important people in Black history and tell who they were/are." Responses were accepted only if sufficient detail was provided about the person listed.

In the domain of personal interests and social behavior there were also favorable changes. The composite variable "social/creative interests" measuring interest in social activity such as rap music and computer games decreased over the course of the program ($t = 2.18$, $p < .05$). Similarly, "creative importance" scores decreased significantly from pre to post test ($t = 3.02$, $p < .01$) suggesting that after program participation, being a good rapper, singer, and musician was less important.

The frequency of after school social behavior/activities diminished as well. "After school social behavior/activities" (e.g., talking on the phone, playing board games & playing with friends) showed a significant decrease ($t = 2.75$, $p < .01$), and the "social importance" composite score indicated a significant decrease ($t = 2.14$, $p < .035$), suggesting that after being in the RAAMUS Academy, being popular with friends, being cool, staying out late, and being a good dancer were not as important anymore. In contrast, mean scores for the variable "self esteem 3" went up (t = 2.19, p < .05) indicating that pro-social attitudes such as getting a good job, helping other people, and not doing drugs were now more important to students.

Grade Point Average

Another primary evaluation of program efficacy consisted of comparisons of student's baseline GPA scores with those following program intervention at 6 months, and 1 year follow up. The literature suggests a gradual decrease in GPA scores for this age group (Reed, 1988) so, at best, a moderate increase in GPA scores was expected. Preliminary findings, while nonsignificant, did reveal a slight increase in mean GPA scores from baseline (M = 2.1; sd. = .78) to 6 month post test (M = 2.2; sd = .79) to 1 year (M = 2.4; sd = .77).

Parent's Feedback

The parent's feedback questionnaire was administered immediately after the program. Response choices were on a four point scale ranging from "very much so" to "not at all." To the question "Did your son appear to enjoy the two-month RAAMUS Academy?", 86% responded "very much so" with a mean response of 3.85. To the question "Do you feel your son learned anything important?", 78% said "very much so" with a mean of 3.8. To the question "Would you recommend this program to a friend?", 96% said "very much so" with a mean of 3.95. To the question "Do you think this program should be continued?", 99% said "very much so" with a mean of 3.95. To the question, "Have you noticed any positive changes in your son?", 44% said "very much so" with another 44% giving the second highest rating of 3 out of 4. For positive changes the mean was 3.21. Consistent with the SQAK results, the open-ended question revealed that positive changes commonly indicated were attitude towards school, self respect, respect for others, cultural awareness, respect for others, and more self discipline.

TABLE 1. Composite variables and t-test results from pre-test and post-test comparisons of the SQAK.

Composite Variable Name	Examples of component items	# Items	Pre-test means	Post-test means	T scores values *	P
Academic Interests	reading, writing, science, math	9	2.73	2.81	1.01	n.s.
Sports Interest	basketball, football, boxing	7	3.09	2.98	.94	n.s.
Social/Creative Interests	rap music, computer games	5	3.43	3.30	2.18	.032*
Self Esteem 1	love myself, love my skin color	5	3.47	3.48	1.61	n.s.
Academic Competence	I am a good reader, good math	13	2.32	2.36	.81	n.s.
Sports Competence	I am a good athlete, a winner	2	2.59	2.54	.89	n.s.
Social Competence	I am cool, I am popular	2	2.35	2.34	.08	n.s.
Creative Competence	I'm a good rapper, singer, creative	4	2.22	2.11	1.81	.08**
Self Esteem 2	I am proud, have good manners	15	2.38	2.45	1.78	.08**
Academic Importance	good grades, good education	5	3.48	3.59	1.57	n.s.
Sports Importance	good fighter, good at sports	3	2.81	2.71	.94	n.s.
Social Importance	being popular, being cool	6	2.58	2.41	2.14	.035*
Creative Importance	good rapper, good singer	3	2.32	2.00	3.02	.003*
Self Esteem 3	helping people, not doing drugs	9	3.54	3.65	2.19	.03*
Freq. Academic Behavior	after school reading, homework	3	.20	.23	3.10	.01*
Freq. Sports Behavior	after school sports, exercise	2	.15	.15	.36	n.s.
Freq. Social Behavior	after school phone talk, friends	3	.64	.62	2.75	.01*
Freq. Creative Behavior	after school hobbies, art, music	3	.19	.19	.75	n.s.
Freq. Personal Behavior	after school TV, music, videos	4	.24	.23	1.38	n.s.
Black History Knowledge	ability to retrieve information	1	3.17	4.08	5.28	.001*

*Significant at P < .05 ** P < .10

To the question "Have you noticed any negative changes in your son?", 75% said "not at all" with a mean of 0.438. When asked to indicate any negative changes that you attribute directly to the program only one parent responded with "he tries to monopolize conversations with talk of Black history in a way to make others feel like they don't know about their history." To the question "Do you want your son to continue participating in the RAAMUS Academy?", 98% said yes. Only one parent said "unsure" indicating that their son was moving out of state.

Another open-ended question was "What did you like most about the Program?" Here, issues around school and cultural awareness made up the bulk of the replies. For example, one parent said "The RAAMUS Academy deserves a standing ovation. My son has gone from a D and F student to a B and C student. We are impressed!" Another said, "It gave my son a positive feeling about his African heritage." To the question, "What did you like least about the Program?", 80% said nothing. Of those who did respond, 72% of the responses were in regards to the short (two month) time frame of the program. For example, one parent wrote "Too short! I would be willing to pay for more advanced sessions." Another wrote, "The program just wasn't long enough. I wish it were on-going until age 18." Other issues mentioned were: meeting on school nights; and recommendations for adding field trips.

DISCUSSION

In this investigation we have developed and assessed a programmatic intervention aimed at providing young African-American males with an alternative set of values regarding education and cultural identity (Ghee, 1994). We predicted that young African-American male students who participated in the RAAMUS Academy would demonstrate increased knowledge of African-American history and cultural identity from pre intervention to post intervention. We also anticipated that they would show increased scholastic motivation, and school performance as a result of participation. The data suggest some potential and promise. Significant pre-post differences were found in student attitudes towards education and in their socio-cultural values. More specifically, the program reduced the importance and frequency of social factors (such as socializing and amusement) and increased the importance and frequency of academic activities in the students' lives. Further, an increase in cultural awareness was evidenced by an increase in knowledge of black history. This model may be effective for young females if it were tailored to their specific sub-cultural needs. The feasibility of the program was evidenced by the positive parent feedback which suggests that this is a desired community based intervention for African-American families.

Study Limitations

This was an exploratory demonstration project. Funding was minimal. Volunteer services and out of pocket expenditures constituted over 60% of administrative resources. While the program targeted lower income "at risk" African-American male youth, the demographic data suggest that most of the families were not in the lower income bracket. Program recruitment was on a first come first serve basis. While it has been argued that all African-American youth are potentially at risk (Gibbs, 1988; Kunjufu, 1988), it is not surprising that many concerned middle income parents took the immediate opportunity to enroll their boys. Another factor may have been that the program required a $50 registration fee and many low income families may not have been able to afford it. Future scrutiny of the data set will attempt to assess differential program impact for low and middle income participants.

The study was a one group pre-post quasi-experiment and thus has numerous threats to internal validity. Our initial intent to secure a matching control group (a community health program) failed when the health program was discontinued one month into the study. However, the supplemental parent's data lend some support for the efficacy and feasibility of the intervention. Another limitation is the inability to follow up with the boys post intervention. While we did conduct periodic booster sessions (called reunions), due to limited resources we were not very successful in providing continuity for the participants after graduation. We do, however, strongly advocate a consistent and longitudinal follow-up protocol for community based edu-cultural programs (Ghee, 1990).

Another limitation was the psychometric properties of the

SQAK. The present analysis is based on a conceptual rather than a statistical clustering of variables. A principle components analysis was used to check the loaded items in each composite. However, conceptual relevant items were still classified into composites based on their correlation with other variables in the composite. For example if "interest in football" did not statistically load with "interest in basketball," or if "love for homework" did not load with "love for studying," the authors classifed items based on conceptual (and cultural) relevance if the correlation coefficient was above .40. This decision may have influenced the results. Nonetheless, reliability coefficients were generally above .60 suggesting at least moderate reliability. The current analyses are based on pre-test and immediate post-test composite scores, thus we do not know if the program has long term value once participants are separated from program support mechanisms and return to the mainstream peer group and negative media influences. Longitudinal follow-up data would address the long term benefits of the program for attitude and behavior change maintenance. We are currently attempting to locate program participants for more extensive follow-up assessment.

A final limitation is in the numerous and multi-modal curriculum activities and strategies. We cannot be sure which curriculum activities worked and which ones did not. We cannot determine whether the youth benefited more from merely receiving attention (interacting with positive role models), from more sophisticated process issues (utilization of music and poetry), or content issues (learning Black History facts). Only a more controlled study delineating and partialling out each of these factors could attempt to answer this question.

The RAAMUS Academy is part of a growing national community action and "Rites of Passage" movement that is providing a small but important voice for those thousands of virtually "invisible" proud and responsible culturally conscious achievers (Watts, 1993). It is consistent with recommendations for strategically using multimedia approaches, which includes elements of Hip-Hop culture, for speaking effectively to and reaching the most alienated of our youth (Watts & Abdul-Adil, 1994; The MEE Report, 1995). This program, like many others, had very limited resources and scope, so it can only be considered exploratory. Future researchers wishing to use the SQAK should evaluate its psychometric properties and proceed with caution until more is known about its validity and reliability as a descriptive or diagnostic tool.

As we move towards the 21st century it is imperative that we create a nationally institutionalized socio-cultural institution for our youth; one that stimulates greater diversity in their occupational aspirations; one that stimulates high achievement motivation; and one that augments their skills acquisitions for individual survival and collective achievement.

REFERENCES

Abdul-Adil, J. (1992). Rap music: Towards a culture-specific paradigm of empowerment. *The Community Psychologist, 26.*

Akbar, N. (1984). *Chains and Images of Psychological Slavery.* Jersey City: New Mind Productions.

Allen, L. & Majidi-Ahi, S. (1989). Black American Children. In Gibbs, & Huang (Eds.), *Children of Color: Psychological Interventions with Minority Youth.* San Francisco:. Jossey-Bass Inc.

Azibo, D. A. (1988). Position Paper: Racial Images in the Media. *Association of Black Psychologist newsletter, 19(4).*

Bell, Y.R. & McGraw-Burrell, R. (1988). Culturally-sensitive and traditional methods of task presentation and learning performance in black children. *Western Journal of Black Studies, 12(4),* 187-193.

Boykin, W. A. (1986). The Triple Quandary and the Schooling of Afro-American Children. In U. Neisser (Ed.), *The school achievement of minority children.* (pp. 57-89). NJ: Lawrence Erlbaum Associates, Inc.

Castinell, L. & Pinar, W. (1993). *Understanding curriculum as racial text.* Albany, NY: State University of New York Press.

Dotter, D. (1987). Growing up is hard to do: Rock and roll performers as cultural heroes. *Sociological Spectrum, 7(1),* 25-44.

Ghee, K.L. (1990). Enhancing educational achievement through cultural awareness in young black males. *The Western Journal of Black Studies, 14(2),*77-89.

Ghee, K.L. (1994). Edu-Culture: An innovative strategy for promoting identity and scholarship in young African American males. In Jones and Borman (Eds.), *The New American schools: Alternative concepts and practices.*

Gibbs, J.T. (1988). Young Black Males in America: Endangered, Embittered, and Embattled. In Gibbs (Ed.), *Young, black, and male in America: An endangered species.* MA: Auburn House Publishing Company.

Hale-Benson, J.E. (1988). *Black children: Their roots, culture, and learning styles.* Baltimore, MD: Johns Hopkins University Press.

Hall, S. (1995).The white of their eyes: Racist ideologies and the media. In Dines, G. & Humez, J. (Eds.), *Gender, race and class in the media: A text reader* (pp. 5-17). Thousand Oaks, CA: Sage Publications Inc.

Hansen, C. (1995). Predicting cognitive and behavioral effects of gangsta rap. *Basic and Applied Social Psychology, 16,* 43-52.

Hilliard, A. (1976). *Alternatives to IQ testing: An approach to the identification of gifted minority children.* San Francisco: San Francisco State University.

Hilliard, A.G. (1985). *Information for excellence and equity in education.* National Center for Educational Statistics.

Johnson, J., Jackson, L. & Gatto, L. (1995). Violent attitudes and deferred academic aspirations: Deleterious effects of exposure to rap music. *Basic and Applied Social Psychology, 16,* 27-41.

Johnson, K. (1991). Objective news and other myths: The poisoning of young black minds. *Journal of Negro Education, 60,* 328-341.

Kellner, D. (1995). Cultural studies, multi-culturalism and media. In Dines, G. & Humez, J. (Eds.), *Gender, race and class in the media: A text reader* (pp. 5-17). Thousand Oaks, CA: Sage Publications Inc.

Korenzy-Felipe, F., McClure, J. & Rzyttki, B. (1990). Ethnicity, communication and drugs. *Journal of Drug Issues, 20,* 87-98.

Kunjufu, J. (1988). *To Be Popular or Smart: The Black Peer Group.* Chicago, IL: African American Images.

Madhubuti, H. (1990). *Black men: Obsolete, single, dangerous?* Chicago: Third World Press.

Nobles, W. (1987). *African American families: Issues, insights and direction.* Oakland, CA.

Reed, R.J. (1988). Education and Achievement in Young Black Males. In Gibbs, J.T. (Ed.), *Young black and male in America: An endangered species* (pp. 37-96). MA: Auburn House Publishing Corp.

Rhodes, J. (1995). The visibility of race and media history. In Dines, G. & Humez, J. (Eds.), *Gender, race and class in the media: A text reader* (pp. 33-39). Thousand Oaks, CA: Sage Publications Inc.

Shade, B. (1982). African American cognitive style: A variable in school success? *The Journal of Black Psychology, 13,* 13-16.

The MEE Report. (1995). *Reaching the Hip-Hop Generation: Executive Summary.* The Robert Wood Johnson Foundation, No. 18762.

Thorndike, E.L. (1939). *Education as cause and as symptom.* New York.

U.S. Department of Commerce. (1990). *Current Population Reports* (Bureau of the Census, Spring, Series No. 32, 70). Washington, DC: U.S. Government Printing Office.

Watts, R. (1993). Community action through manhood development: A look at concepts and concerns from the front line. *American Journal of Community Psychology, 21.* 333-359.

Watts, R. & Abdul-Adil, J. (1994). Psychological aspects of oppression and socio-political development: Building young warriors. In R. Newby & T. Manley (Eds.), *The poverty of inclusion, innovation and interventions: The dilemma of the African-American underclass.* Rutgers, NJ: Rutgers University Press.

Wilson, C. & Gutirrez, F. (1995). *Race, multi-culturalism & the media: From mass to class communication* (2nd ed.):Thousand Oaks, CA: Sage Publications.

Wlodkowski, R.J. & Jaynes, J.H. (1990). *Eager to Learn: Helping Children Become Motivated and Love Learning.* NJ: Jossey-Bass Inc.

Woodson, C. (1933). *Miseducation of the Negro.* Washington, DC: Assoc. Publishers.

The Spiritual Well-Being of African-Americans: A Preliminary Analysis

Jacqueline S. Mattis

University of Michigan

SUMMARY. This multi-method study explored the relationship between gender, spirituality, spiritual well-being, and several indices of religiosity including religious participation and religious motivation. Different patterns of relationships among these indices emerged for men and women. For men Spiritual Well-Being was related to the presence and influence of church-oriented socializing agents as well as to the belief in God's power to influence the course of events. Mean scores on measures of the importance of religion, current religious participation, religious motivation, as well as spiritual well-being were not significantly different for men and women. *[Article copies available for a fee from The Haworth Document Delivery Service: 1-800-342-9678. E-mail address: getinfo@haworth.com]*

For four decades scholars interested in the psychology of religion have grappled with the complex relationships between the cognitive, affective and experiential dimensions of religion and spirituality. Empirical research has examined the relationship between religiosity, spirituality and a range of psychological variables including coping (Pargament, Ensing, Falgout, Olsen, Reilly, Van

---

[Haworth co-indexing entry note]: "The Spiritual Well-Being of African-Americans: A Preliminary Analysis." Mattis, Jacqueline S. Co-published simultaneously in *Journal of Prevention & Intervention in the Community* (The Haworth Press, Inc.) Vol. 16, No. 1/2, 1997, pp. 103-120; and: *Manhood Development in Urban African-American Communities* (ed: Roderick J. Watts, and Robert J. Jagers) The Haworth Press, Inc., 1997, pp. 103-120. Single or multiple copies of this article are available for a fee from The Haworth Document Delivery Service [1-800-342-9678, 9:00 a.m. - 5:00 p.m. (EST). E-mail address: getinfo@haworth.com].

Haitsma & Warren, 1990), and well-being (Koenig, 1995). Within the small body of empirical research on the psychology of religion is an even smaller body of work on the religious and spiritual experiences of African-Americans. This latter body of research has consistently found that African-American women score higher than African-American men on measures of religious participation, affiliation, salience, commitment, subjective religiosity and spirituality (Levin, Taylor, & Chatters, 1995; Taylor & Chatters, 1991; Taylor, 1988; Neighbors, Jackson, Bowman, & Gurin, 1983; Jagers & Smith, 1996). African-American women also are more likely than men to use prayer as a key strategy for coping with adversity (Levin & Taylor, 1993; Neighbors et al., 1983). These findings maintain across the developmental span (Donahue & Benson, 1995).

The ubiquity of empirical evidence which signals gender differences in religious experiences and behaviors have led some researchers to conclude that women are simply more religious than are men (Taylor, 1991). However, there continues to be a need to systematically study the scope and substance of these gender differences. At present the field continues to reify findings which suggest that women are more religious than men, even while it remains virtually mute about the religious and spiritual profile of African-American men. There is a need for iterations about the specific experiences, conditions and factors which positively shape the religious development of African-American men. There is a need to explore the extent to which there may be gender differences in men and women's beliefs about God, as well as differences in men and women's perceptions about the function(s) of religion and spirituality in their lives. In addition, it is important to assess whether or not these gender differences have implications for men and women's perceptions of their well-being.

Studies conducted across the developmental span have demonstrated that religion and spirituality promote psychological well-being, and mitigate against negative social outcomes (Potts, 1991). In their review of empirical research on the relationship between religiosity and well-being, Donahue and Benson (1995) found that religiosity was negatively related to substance abuse, early sexual involvement, delinquent behavior and suicidality among adolescents. Similarly, in their work with a sample of sixth grade inner-city African-American youth, Jagers and Mock (1993) found that a spiritual orientation was associated with fewer reported acts of delinquency. Further, Jagers and Mock (1993) found that a spiritual orientation was positively associated with the demonstration of pro-social values and behaviors. In their research, Maton and Wells (1995) found that adolescents who were mentored by church-involved individuals were significantly more likely to have higher school grades and fewer school withdrawals than those who were mentored by individuals in secular settings.

These findings suggest that the inculcation of religious and spiritual values may be important to preventive intervention efforts. A religious or spiritual orientation may be crucial to the prevention of antisocial behaviors, and other negative life outcomes among young men and women. Equally important, these orientations may be important for the development of such positive social values as interpersonal cooperation (Jagers, Smith, Mock and Dill, forthcoming). In addition, Maton and Wells' (1995) findings suggest that it is not simply the individual's direct experience of religion or spirituality that is important. Interactions with socializing agents who are church-involved may be important for enhancing the well-being of young people. The extent to which these findings hold true for urban-residing, college-age African-Americans remains largely unexplored, however.

The focal concern of this study was to elucidate gender differences in religiosity and spirituality among young, urban residing African-American men and women. "Religiosity" and "spirituality" are defined here as distinct but confluent domains of human life. Religion (e.g., Islam, Christianity, Judaism) is understood as a shared system of beliefs about a deity or set of deities which is formalized into philosophies, practices and written doctrines (e.g., the Quran, the Bible, the Torah). "Religiosity," by extension, is defined as an individual's degree of adherence to the beliefs, doctrines and practices of a particular religion. In contrast, spirituality is defined as "the acceptance of or belief in the sacred force that resides in all things" life (Potts, 1991). The belief in a shared essence has implications for individuals' notions about the interconnectedness of all forms of life, as well as beliefs about a vast array of responsibilities which individuals have to proximal and distal others (Jagers & Smith, 1996). Religiosity is one manifestation of a spiritual orientation (Jagers & Smith, 1996). However, it is feasible that an individual who does not adhere to the tenets of any religious doctrine might, nevertheless, believe in the sacredness of all living things.

This research explored gender differences in seven domains of religious and spiritual experience. First, the study explored gender differences in the functions of religion in early and current life. Second, it explored differences in patterns of religious participation early in life as well as in their current lives. Third, the study examined differences in men and women's reports about the early and present importance of religious beliefs to their households. Fourth, gender differences in religious motivation were explored. Three dimensions of religious motivation were examined. These dimensions examine the extent to which individuals are motivated by faith (internal motivation), by their relationships with religious others (external motivation), and/or by their need to grapple with existential questions and doubts (quest motivation). Fifth, the study examined differences in men and women's cognitions about God's capacity to effect changes in the lives of individuals. Sixth, gender differences in spiritual orientation were explored.

Finally, the study explored the extent to which these factors affect the well-being of men and women. In contrast with other studies which measure well-being in terms of physical health outcomes (Koenig, 1995) or psychological health outcomes (Blaine & Crocker, 1995), this study attended to spiritual well-being (see Ellison, 1983). This study privileged a definition of spiritual well-being which comprises individuals' experiences of security in their relationships with God, and their feelings of satisfaction and contentment with their life trajectories (Ellison, 1983).

Empirical findings of gender differences in patterns of religious behavior and in subjective religiosity (see Levin, Taylor & Chatters, 1995) suggest that religion may function differently for men and women. As such, it is expected that the qualitative data will reveal gender differences in the early and current functions of religion. Previous research has demonstrated that African-American college age men and women score higher than their European-American counterparts on measures of spiritual orientation, internal, external and quest orientations, as well as the belief in the causal agency of God (Jagers & Smith, 1996). In keeping with the findings of previous studies it was anticipated that women would score higher than their male counterparts on all measures of religiosity and spirituality. That is, in this study it was expected that African-American women would score higher than their male counter parts on measures of religious participation, perceived importance of religion, religious motivation, beliefs about the causal agency of God, spiritual orientation and spiritual well-being. While this research is comparative in nature particular efforts were made to highlight the factors which affect the spiritual well-being of men. The implications of this work for interventions with young African-American men and women are discussed.

METHOD

Participants

Sixty-eight (27 male and 41 female) African-Americans were recruited from introductory psychology courses at a large university located in an urban setting in the Midwest. Participation in this study served as partial fulfillment of a requirement for these introductory psychology courses. Participants had a mean age of 21.1 years, (SD = 3.20) and a mean level of education of 14.7 years.

Measures

Functions of Religion/Religiosity. Two open-ended questions were asked which allowed us to assess the "functional significance of religion" in the lives of participants: "What were the most important things that your beliefs did or did not do for you while you were growing up?" and "What are the most important things that your beliefs do or do not do for you currently?" Participants provided three responses to each of these questions. Each participant rank-ordered their three responses with their first response indicating the most important subjective function of religion, and the third response being the least important function of their religious beliefs.

Religious Participation was assessed using two items: "How often did you participate in formal religious services while growing up?" and "How often do you participate in formal religious services?" These items were scored on a five point scale (1= not at all to 5 = more than once a week).

Importance of Religion. The importance of religious beliefs in the early and current lives of respondents was assessed by means of two close-ended questions: "How important were religious beliefs in your home while you were growing up?" and "How important are your religious beliefs in your life currently?" Both questions were scored on a four point scale (1 = not important at all to 4 = very important).

The Religious Life Inventory (Batson, 1976) is a 27 item measure of three crucial dimensions of religious/spiritual motivation: Internal religious motivation, External religious motivation and a Quest motivation. Items on the RLI are measured on a nine-point scale ranging from strongly agree (1) to strongly disagree (9). An Internal motivation reflects the extent to which one's personal identity and one's self-concept revolve around one's faith in God (example: "I find it impossible to conceive of myself as not being religious."). The External orientation to religion reflects the extent to which significant others have influenced one's religious development (example: "My minister (Sunday school teacher, youth director, etc.) has had a profound influence on my personal religious development"). The Quest orientation reflects one's efforts to grapple with religious questions and doubts (example: "Questions are far more important to my religious experience than are answers"). Studies have yielded alpha coefficients of .80, .60 and .63 for the internal, external and quest scales respectively (see Jagers & Smith, 1996).

God as Causal Agent Scale (Ritzema & Young, 1983) is a 14 item scale which assesses the extent to which individuals attribute the cause of events to the intervention of God. The scale includes seven items which make direct causal attributions to God (example: "Every new life is a direct miracle of God."). The remaining seven items, which are reverse scored, proffer non-theistic causes for events (example: "I have never been completely sure that anything that has happened in my life has come as an answer to prayer."). The items of the GCAS are measured on a 5-point scale (1 = strongly disagree to 5 = strongly agree). An alpha-coefficient of .74 has been reported for the GCAS (Jagers & Smith, 1996). Participants in this study achieved a mean of 3.5 (*SD* = .60).

The Spiritual Orientation Scale (SOS) developed by Jagers, Boykin and Smith (1996) assesses individuals' beliefs in the sacredness and transcendent nature of life. This scale assesses both the philosophical and the behavioral dimensions of spirituality (Jagers et al., 1996). Among its items are "All people have a common core which is sacred," and "Though I may go to the doctor when I am ill, I also pray." The 25 items on this measure are scored on a six-point scale (1 = completely false to 6 = completely true). Studies using this scale with African-American college students have generated alpha coefficients ranging from .83 to .87 (Jagers & Smith, 1996).

The *Spiritual Well-Being Scale* was developed by Ellison (1983) as a 20-item measure of religious commitment, beliefs about the transcendent nature of life, the quality of the individual's relationship with God, and individuals' sense of purpose and meaning in life. An advantage of this index is that it assesses spiritual well-being independently of adherence to any specific system of religious belief. The 20 items of the Spiritual Well-Being Scale (SWB) are divided into a religious and an existential dimension of well-being. The religious dimension of well-being is comprised of 10 items which use the individual's relationship to God as a central referent in the evaluation of well-being (example: "My relationship with God helps me not to feel lonely"). The 10 items which measure the existential dimension of well-being do not reference God or religion (example: "I feel good about my future"). Spiritual Well-Being (SWB), in short, is measured as a composite of the religious and existential dimensions of well-being. Summary scores for SWB were calculated by summing and averaging responses to items on the scale. Ellison (1983) reports an alpha coefficient of .87 for the SWB scale.

Procedures

Two trained independent raters coded the written narrative responses to the two open-ended questions about the function of religion in their lives. An open-coding approach (Strauss & Corbin, 1990) was used in the coding of the narratives. That is, the data were coded without use of a priori categories. Instead, the categories were constructed during systematic review of the written responses. The categories reflect respondents' statements about the functions of religion and spirituality in their lives. Eight coding categories emerged from these narrative responses. The eight categories are: (1) fostering positive values, (2) promotion of self-development, (3) providing explanations for crucial life events or existential concerns, (4) facilitating efforts to cope, (5) facilitation of interpersonal relationships, (6) provision of behavioral constraint, (7) conflict management and (8) doctrinal information.

RESULTS

Functional Significance of Religiosity

There were virtually no gender differences in the functions of religion in the early lives of men and women. Male and female respondents indicated that the most important roles of religious beliefs in their early lives were to promote positive values, influence self-development, and to assist them in exercising behavioral constraint (see Table 1).

There were gender differences in the functions of religion in the current lives of African-American men and women (see Table 2). Thirty-seven percent (37%) of the men and 15% of the women identified religion as being important in fostering positive values in their lives at present. Twenty-two percent of the female respondents identified self-development as the most important current function of religion for them. None of the male respondents endorsed this category.

Quantitative Analyses

African-American women were significantly more likely than their male cognates to participate in religious services early in life

TABLE 1. Summary of Qualitative Analysis of the Most Important Early Life Functions of Religious Beliefs (N = 68)

Category	Most Important Male (n = 27)	Most Important Female (n = 41)
1. Positive Values	26%	22%
2. Self-Development	22%	19%
3. Explanations	4%	4%
4. Coping	4%	7%
5. Interpersonal	4%	7%
6. Behavioral Constraint	19%	7%
7. Conflict	7%	7%
8. Doctrinal	7%	7%

TABLE 2. Most Important Current Functions of Religious Beliefs (N = 68)

Category	Most Important Males (n = 27)	Most Important Females (n = 41)
1. Positive Values	37%	15%
2. Self-Development	0%	22%
3. Explanations	4%	0%
4. Coping	11%	19%
5. Interpersonal	0%	15%
6. Behavioral Constraint	11%	0%
7. Conflict	11%	4%
8. Doctrinal	11%	4%

t (66) = 2.04, $p < .05$). However, no gender difference emerged in current participation in religious services. Analyses also indicated that there were no gender differences in early or current importance of religion in the households of these men and women. These findings suggest that despite the differential patterns of early involvement in religious activities, men did not differ from women in their perceptions of the importance of religion to their families.

Women were more likely than men to endorse an internal orientation to religiosity t (66) = 2.06, $p < .05$. However, there was no significant difference in men and women's scores on the external or quest dimensions of religiosity. These findings indicate that African-American women were more likely than men to express a need for faith and certainty. However, men and women do not differ in their reports about the importance of social others in their religious development or in their pursuit of answers to religious doubts and questions.

Women scored higher than their male counterparts on the God as a Causal Agent Scale t (65) = 2.05, p < .05), indicating that they were more likely than men to attribute events to the power and creative intervention of God.

T-tests revealed no significant difference in the mean spiritual orientation scores of men and women. While women's mean endorsements of the GCAS measure were significantly higher, however, women's belief in God's causal power was not associated with any other indices of religiosity or spirituality. For African-American males, however, the belief God's causal influence in life events was strongly associated with both an internal religious orientation (r = .60; p < .01) and a spiritual orientation (r = 53, p < .01) (see Table 3). In short, men who believe that God influences the events which occur in the world were also likely to see their faith in God as central to their identity, and to believe that all living things share a vital essence.

For male respondents there was a moderate relationship between the Internal and External religious motivation (r = .45, p < .05). There was no significant relationship between the Internal and External religious motivation for women. This finding suggests that for African-American men, but not for women, the presence of religious socializing agents is associated with the tendency to see their faith in God as central to their personal identity. Neither of these motivational orientations was significantly correlated with the Quest motivation for men or women (see Tables 3 and 4).

The Internal orientation was strongly correlated with spiritual orientation for both males (r = .50, p < .01) and females (r = .52, p < .01). As such, for both men and women the importance of faith to one's experience of self is positively related to one's belief that all living things share a vital, sacred essence.

Male respondents had a mean Spiritual Well-Being score of 4.55 (SD = .57) while their female counterparts had a mean score of 4.47 (SD = .76) on this measure. There was no significant difference between these mean scores. However, the patterns of relationship between well-being and the religiosity indices were different for men and women. For African-American males the belief in the

TABLE 3. Correlations Between Religiosity and Spirituality Variables for African-American Men (n = 27)

	GCAS	RLI (I)	RLI (E)	RLI(Q)	SWB	SOS
GCAS	--					
RLI (I)	.60**	--				
RLI (E)	.26	.45*	--			
RLI (Q)	.01	.03	.00	--		
SWB	.40*	.19	.50**	.01	--	
SOS	.53**	.50**	.31	−.16	.27	--

* *p* < .05, ** *p* < .01

TABLE 4. Correlations Between Religiosity and Spirituality Variables for African-American Women (n = 41)

	GCAS	RLI (I)	RLI (E)	RLI (Q)	SWB	SOS
GCAS	--					
RLI (I)	.19	--				
RLI (E)	.15	.18	--			
RLI (Q)	.16	.23	−.24	--		
SWB	.12	.26	.46**	−.11	--	
SOS	.29	.52**	.33*	.12	.58**	--

* *p* .05, ** *p* < .01

causal agency of God was significantly related to Spiritual Well-Being ($r = .40$, $p < .01$). In addition, the Spiritual Well-Being of African-American men was moderately associated with the presence of external socializing agents in their lives ($r = .50$, $p < .01$). For African-American women Spiritual Well-Being was associated with spiritual orientation ($r = .58$, $p < .01$) and with the influence of external socializing agents ($r = .46$, $p < .01$). These results suggest that for both men and women spiritual well-being is informed by the presence of religious or church-involved individuals in their lives. However, while women's spiritual well-being is associated with a belief that all living things share a vital essence, for men, spiritual well-being is associated with the belief that God plays a role in shaping events and circumstances.

Post-hoc analyses were conducted to examine the extent to which gender, belief in God's causal influence, spiritual orientation and religious motivation might predict spiritual well-being of African-Americans. Gender, as well as summary scores for the GCAS, Spiritual Orientation Scale and of the External (RLI(E)), Internal (RLI(I)) and Quest (RLI(Q)) religious motivation measures were entered as a block into a regression equation as predictors of Spiritual Well-Being (see Table 5).

The regression model predicting Spiritual Well-Being was significant (adjusted R^2 = .26, p < .01). Gender failed to emerge as a significant predictor of Spiritual Well-Being. However, spiritual orientation and the experience of having relationships with church-involved others (RLI(E)) were predictive of Spiritual Well-Being.

DISCUSSION

The present study examined the functions of religion in early as well as present life. In addition, the study examined patterns of relationship between men and women's religious participation, beliefs about the importance of religion, religious motivation, beliefs about the power of God, spiritual orientation and their experience of spiritual well-being. This approach to the study of religiosity is consistent with the multi-dimensional approach suggested by Levin, Taylor and Chatters (1995). Levin et al. suggest that religiosity should be understood as a synthesis of experiences, values, behaviors, relationships and beliefs.

TABLE 5. Summary of Standard Multiple Regression Analysis for Variables Predicting Spiritual Well-Being Scores

Variable	B	SE B	β
Gender	.12	.16	.08
GCAS	.03	.14	.02
RLI (I)	− .03	.07	− .06
RLI (E)	.21	.06	.37
RLI (Q)	.01	.06	.01
SOS	.38	.14	.36*

Adj R^2 = .26*
* p < .01, *** p < .0001

The hypothesized relationships between gender and many of the indices of religiosity and spirituality were borne out by the results of this study. Women scored significantly higher than men on measures of early participation in religious activities and services, internal religious motivation, and belief in God's power to influence the direction of life events. In contrast to hypothesized findings, women did not score higher than men on measures of current church attendance, external or quest religious motivation, perceived importance of religion, or spiritual well-being. These findings were generally consistent with the findings of previous research which suggest that women are more religious and more spiritual than men (Levin, Taylor, & Chatters, 1995; Jagers & Smith, 1996). However, this work also demonstrated that the relationship between gender, religiosity and spirituality is not a simple one. The assertion that women are more religious than their male counterparts may be premature. At present much of the work on the psychology of religion has centered on quantifiable phenomena and on the differences between men and women's scores on measures of religiosity and spirituality. However, we must position ourselves to ask different and increasingly complex questions about religious and spiritual development. We must broaden our approach by asking how men and women experience, express and use religiosity and spirituality. We must begin to explore the ways in which gender socialization may affect the men and women's expressions and experiences of their religious and spiritual sensibilities. In addition, we must begin to attend to the ways in which men and women use their religious and spiritual beliefs to construct meaning (Mattis, under review).

The results of this study elucidate important directions for inquiry into the religious and spiritual lives of young African-Americans, however, its limitations must be acknowledged. The study is delimited by the small size of this sample. In addition, the high level of educational attainment of the sample limits the generalizability of these findings to other African-American men and women. Taken together, these limitations suggest the need for interpretive caution.

This study of religiosity and spirituality would not be complete without a brief consideration of its implications for preventive interventions. The findings of this research suggest that preventive interventions should have two guiding concerns. First, the findings of this study suggest that intervention programs which seek to promote religious as well as existential well-being (i.e., spiritual well-being) in African-American males should highlight God's capacity to intercede in and cause changes in life events. Second, the results of the study suggest that programs should seek to establish relationships between young men and religiously and spiritually oriented others. It is reasonable to speculate that relationships with such individuals provide the context in which to explore new values, and synthesize those new values into coherent worldviews. This latter point should not be misinterpreted as a tacit endorsement of "church-sponsored" or "church-based" programs of intervention. Churches which do not have the commitment, infrastructure, administrative competence or professional grounding necessary to run effective preventive intervention programs, will not be effective agents of change. Whether they are secular or religious in their orientation, programs of intervention which are concerned with promoting the spiritual well-being of young African-American men and women, should be relationship-centered.

The relationships which are fostered in such programs must be substantive ones. If preventive intervention programs are to be effective in achieving long-term changes in the lives of young African-American men and women program developers must have a clear understanding of the relational lives of these young people. As such, one direction for future research might be the exploration of the ways in which core values are transmitted, reinforced and maintained in the peer group and hierarchical relationships of young African-American people. The relationships which are fostered as a part of the preventive intervention programs must address or be compatible with the relational needs and styles of the young people being served by the program(s). Programs which are directed towards meeting the need of marginalized or socially isolated youth also must provide these young people with opportunities to develop the core interpersonal and social skills which will allow them to effectively initiate and maintain relationships with other members of the community.

Intervention and prevention oriented programs must appreciate that the mere conveyance of new or seemingly important values to young people may not be enough to initiate or sustain change. The values which are transmitted to adolescents through relationships will be sustained only if they can be translated into behaviors which are effective in addressing relevant life demands. Values which are useful only in an "ideal world" will be experienced by adolescents as sentimental and inert. As such, preventive intervention programs must do more than transmit core, ideal values. These programs must help young people to translate core values into concrete life skills.

While relationships appear to be important to the religious and spiritual development of young people, intervention and prevention programs must begin to critically examine the value of various models of relationship. At present, intervention programs typically follow a relationship model in which program participants are the sole or primary beneficiaries of the altruism of others. However, research conducted by Apfel and Simon (1996) suggest that children who live under conditions of chronic, traumatic stress and who engage in helping activities (i.e., delivering food to neighbors) were more resilient than their counterparts who did not engage in such activities. Apfel and Simon's findings suggest that adolescents may benefit from relationships in which they provide instrumental help and comfort to others.

Non-reciprocal ("self"-centered) relationships may reinforce patterns of entitlement and selfishness. In contrast, other-directed helping relationships may provide venues in which young people can grapple with and perhaps resolve questions about the meaning or meaningfulness of life (their own as well as the lives of others). Through other-directed, helping relationships, young people may develop clear ideas about the interconnectedness of life, as well as about their responsibilities to others. Further, they may gain a vision of themselves as nurturing and life-sustaining beings. In short, for young people, other-centered helping relationships may serve as vital bridges to more constructive and sustainable personal and communal orientations.

Future research should investigate the impact of gender on an ever broader array of religiosity and spirituality variables. For example, there is a need for the empirical study of gender differences in the religious socialization of African-Americans. Future research may also benefit from longitudinal examinations of religious and spiritual development. Such an approach will allow researchers to map the patterns of change in religious and spiritual beliefs, practices, and experiences which occur across the life span of men and women in specific points of transition in development.

In addition, special attention must be given to the study of the interpersonal as well as intra-personal factors which facilitate the well-being of African-American men and women. We must raise questions about the kinds of relationships which may be most useful for interventions with African-American adolescents. For example, we must address questions about the extent to which core moral values can be effectively transferred in transient relationships (i.e., time-limited relationships with mentors and/or instructors). That is, are transient relationships effective venues for transmitting core values to young people who do not have the familial and other supports necessary to reinforce those values? This question is particularly relevant for those who provide interventions to young people who are socially or emotionally isolated or marginalized. With the use of increasingly sophisticated qualitative and quantitative data gathering and data analytic techniques, these complex studies of the religious and spiritual development will become more feasible.

REFERENCES

Apfel, R. J. & Simon, B. (1996). Psychosocial Interventions for Children of War: The Value of a Model of Resiliency. *Medicine and Global Survival,* 3: A2.

Batson, C. D. & Ventis, W. L. (1982). *The Religious Experience: A Social-Psychological Perspective.* New York: Oxford University Press.

Batson, C. D. (1976). Religion as Pro-social: Agent or Double Agent? *Journal for the Scientific Study of Religion,* 15, 29-45.

Billingsley, A. & Caldwell, C. H. (1991). The Church, the Family, and the School in the African American Community. *Journal of Negro Education, 60,* 427-440.

Blaine, B. & Crocker, J. (1995). Religiousness, Race and Psychological-Well-Being: Exploring Social Psychological Indicators. *Personality and Social Psychology Bulletin,* 21, 1,031-1,041.

Caldwell, C. H. (1994). Social Science Functions of the Contemporary Black Church: Findings From the Black Church Family Project. In Robert J. Taylor and Charlene Flagg (Eds.), *African American Research Perspectives,* Winter 1994, Vol. 1, No. 1, 9-14.

Cone, J. (1986). *Speaking the Truth: Ecumenism, Liberation and Black Theology.* Grand Rapids, Michigan: William B. Eerdmans.

Donahue, M. J. and Benson, P. L. (1995). Religion and the Well-Being of Adolescents. *Journal of Social Issues,* Vol. 51, No. 2, 145-160.

Ellison, C. (1983). Spiritual Well-Being: Conceptualization and Measurement. *Journal of Psychology and Theology,* Vol. 11, No. 4, 330-340.

Jagers, R. J. & Mock, L. O. (1993). Culture and Social Outcomes Among Inner-City African American Children: An Afrographic Exploration. *Journal of Black Psychology,* Vol. 19, No. 4, 391-405.

Jagers, R. J. & Smith, P. (1996). Further Examination of the Spirituality Scale. *Journal of Black Psychology,* Vol. 22, No. 4, 429-442.

Jagers, R. J., Smith, P., Mock, L. O. & Dill, E. (1996). An Afrocultural Social Ethos: Component Orientations and Some Social Implications. Unpublished manuscript. University of Illinois at Chicago.

Koenig, G. (1995). Religion and Health in Later Life. In M. Kimble, S. McFadden, J. Ellor, and J. Seeber (Eds.), *Aging, Spirituality and Religion: A Handbook.* Minneapolis: Fortress Press.

Kunnie, J. (1994). *Models of Black Theology: Issues in Class, Culture and Gender.* Valley Forge, PA: Trinity Press International.

Levin, J. & Taylor, R. (1993). Gender and Age Differences Among Black Americans. *The Gerontologist,* 33, 16-23.

Levin, J., Taylor, R. & Chatters, L. (1995). A Multidimensional Measure of Religious Involvement for African Americans. *The Sociological Quarterly,* Vol. 36, No. 1, 157-173.

Maton, K. & Wells, E. (1995). Religion as a Community Resource for Well-Being: Prevention, Healing, and Empowerment Pathways. *Journal of Social Issues,* Vol. 51, No. 2, 177-193.

Mattis, J. (Under Review). Workings of the Spirit: Spirituality Coping and Transcendence in the Lives of African American Women. University of Michigan.

McKay, N. Y. (1989). Nineteenth-Century Black Women's Spiritual Autobiographies: Religious Faith and Self-Empowerment. In Personal Narratives Group (Eds.), *Interpreting Womens Lives: Feminist Theory and Personal Narrative.* Bloomington: Indiana University Press.

McCarthy Brown, K. (1991). *Mama Lola: A Vodou Priestess in Brooklyn.* Berkeley: University of California Press.

Neighbors, H., Jackson, J., Bowman, P. & Gurin, G. (1983). *Stress, Coping, and Black Mental Health: Preliminary Findings From a National Study.* Newbury Park, Ca.: Sage Publications.

Pargament, K., Ensing, D., Falgout, K., Olsen, H., Reilly, B., Van Haitsma, K., & Warren, R. (1990). God Help Me: (I): Religious Coping as Predictors of the Outcomes of Significant Negative Life Events. *American Journal of Community Psychology,* Vol. 18, N. 6, 793-824.

Potts, R. (1991). Spirits in the Bottle: Spirituality and Alcoholism Treatment in African American Communities. *Journal of Training and Practice in Professional Psychology,* 5, 53-64.

Ritzema, R. J. & Young, C. (1983). Causal Schemata and the Attribution of Supernatural Causality. *Journal of Psychology and Theology,* 11, 36-43.

Strauss, A. and Corbin, J. (1990). *Basics of Qualitative Research: Grounded Theory Procedures and Techniques.* Newbury Park, Ca.: Sage Publications.

Taylor, R. J. (1986). Religious Participation Among Elderly Blacks. *The Gerontologist, 26,* 630-636.

Taylor, R. J. (1988). Correlates of Religious Non-Involvement Among Black Americans. *Review of Religious Research,* Vol. 29, No. 4, 126-139.

Taylor, R. J. and Chatters, L. M. (1991). Religious Life. In James Jackson (Ed.), *Life In Black America.* Newbury Park, CA: Sage Publications.

Tinney, J. S. (1981). The Religious Experience of Black Men. In Lawrence E. Gary (Ed.), *Black Men.* Newbury Park, CA: Sage Publications.

Williams, D. R. (1994). The measurement of Religion in Epidemiologic Studies: Problems and Prospects. In Jefferey S. Levin (Ed.), *Religion in Aging and Health: Theoretical Foundations and Methodological Frontiers.* Thousand Oaks, CA: Sage Publications.

The Balance and Connection
of Manhood and Womanhood Training

Nsenga Warfield-Coppock

Baobab Associates, Inc.

SUMMARY. In this article, African cosmology was a foundation for the exploration of ancient, traditional and contemporary manhood and womanhood training, as well as the connection between them. Laws of nature and the interdependence of universal elements established an African centered or Optimal conceptualization system that eliminated dichotomies based on a Eurocentric (sub-optimal) cosmology. Examples from nature illustrated the complementarity of opposites, the balance of spiritual energies, and the connection of male and female forces. Socialization for females and men, using rites of passage was placed in a wider community context of respiritualization. Practices of transition and transformation, as well as significant familial roles throughout the life cycle in traditional African and contemporary African-American settings were discussed. A four-step model for current day reafrikanization was presented: rediscovery, redefinition, revitalization and restoration. These stages served as a guide to the strategies and practices needed to provide positive cultural identity and balanced interpersonal relationships for people of African descent. *[Article copies available for a fee from The Haworth Document Delivery Service: 1-800-342-9678. E-mail address: getinfo@haworth.com]*

[Haworth co-indexing entry note]: "The Balance and Connection of Manhood and Womanhood Training." Warfield-Coppock, Nsenga. Co-published simultaneously in *Journal of Prevention & Intervention in the Community* (The Haworth Press, Inc.) Vol. 16, No. 1/2, 1997, pp. 121-145; and: *Manhood Development in Urban African-American Communities* (ed: Roderick J. Watts, and Robert J. Jagers) The Haworth Press, Inc., 1997, pp. 121-145. Single or multiple copies of this article are available for a fee from The Haworth Document Delivery Service [1-800-342-9678, 9:00 a.m. - 5:00 p.m. (EST). E-mail address: getinfo@haworth.com].

121

INTRODUCTION:
THE FEMININE AND MASCULINE
CONCEPTUAL FRAMEWORK

African cosmology serves as a foundation for our exploration of manhood and womanhood and the means by which African people have achieved their status traditionally and currently. Unlike members of societies founded on European cosmology, in which adult status is ascribed simply because of age, Africans maintain that appropriate values and moral conduct are necessary for the privilege and distinction of being considered an adult. Youth of African descent can benefit from an African centered map that allows all people to develop individually while creating an optimal environment for the continuation of African people and their cultural institutions (family, traditional spiritual groups, and female and male fraternal societies). Establishing these institutions requires an understanding of the connection between their continuance and manhood and womanhood socialization (training).

Universal laws[1] (see King, 1990; King, Dixon, & Nobles, 1976; Mbiti, 1989; Serequeberhan, 1991) are a contextual framework for understanding the ancient and traditional ways of African peoples. We begin with a clarification of the male-female link based on the laws of nature and the interdependence of universal elements. In African cosmology, the masculine-feminine connection is part of the balance of spiritual energies. It includes the laws of the complementarity of opposites and the balance between the visible and invisible worlds. African cosmology is ruled by laws of cycles and complementarity of opposites. Sets of opposite characteristics include elements like, "talking and keeping silent," "caution and courage," "humility and self-confidence," or "indifference and love," representing two complementary manifestations of the same force. When one is manifest, the other remains unmanifest in the unity of opposites (Haich, 1974). For example, good and evil arise through the separation of unity. However, unity itself is neither good nor evil, but divine. When elements are separated one can recognize them as complementary opposites–hence the Hausa tale, "Life and Death":

Two old men named Life and Death journeyed together and came upon a spring. They asked the owner of the spring for permission to drink. He said yes, but as is custom, said "let the elder drink first." Life and Death quarreled back and forth about who was the elder and should drink first. Finally, they asked the spring's owner to judge the disagreement. He said: "How can one speak of Death without Life, from which it proceeds? And how can one speak of Life without Death, to which all living things go? Both of you have spoken eloquently. Your words are true. Neither can exist without the other . . . Life and death are merely two faces [masks] of the Creator. Therefore you are of equal age. Here is a gourd of water. Drink from it together." (Courlander, 1996, pp. 56-57)

According to this tale, opposites walk together, each dependent on the other for their very existence. If one was not recognizable in separation from the other they could not exist at all. So it is with the feminine and the masculine–two faces of the same Creator, one complementing the other, one existing only because of the other, neither one junior nor senior to the other, walking together forever throughout eternity.

While it becomes clear that each face serves as a mask for the other, each serves as a complement because the feminine and the masculine have distinct energy, intensity, and etiology. Complementarity, separation, and balance of the masculine and feminine has its foundation in ancient human history. The physical manifestation of masculine and feminine energies are found in the customs and lessons given boys and girls. This perspective suggests that the return to African harmony requires a collective journey through the life cycle, reafrikanization through rites of passage, and mastering essential male (son, brother, husband, father, grandfather) and female (daughter, sister, wife, mother, grandmother) roles.

Linda James Myers (1988; 1991) reminds us that the ancient Africans based their wisdom on self-knowledge rooted in symbolic imagery and rhythm. This conceptual system (Optimal Psychology) eliminates the dichotomies that exist in the Eurocentric (sub-optimal) system of conceptualization which relies only on the material reality–external "truth," the acquisition of property, knowledge based on counting and measuring, etc. In other words following a Eurocentric blueprint serves only to hinder and seriously compromise our ability to recreate an Afrikan reality. The benefit of the optimal system, which is a union of opposites, including, at the same time, the visible and invisible, promotes the positive cultural identity and balanced interpersonal relationships in people of African descent (Myers, 1991; 1994). These concepts guide us to strategies and practices to renew our wisdom and expertise in the development of African man and womanhood. Of essential importance is the knowledge which supports the return to partnership and equality, reciprocity, harmony and respect–things Africans traditionally enjoyed.

The Complementarity of Nature and Humans

Observations and messages from nature illustrate and teach the spiritual connection of humans (male and female) in the scheme of all that is spirit and in balance. As an aid to understanding the importance of the balance and complementarity of nature and humans, we offer an illustrative poem penned by Anita Scott Coleman (1931): which originally appeared in the June, 1931, issue of *The Crisis*.

Portraiture

Black men are the tall trees that remain
Standing in a forest after a fire.
Flames strip their branches,
Flames sear their limbs.
Flames scorch their trunks.
Yet stand these trees
For their roots are thrust deep
In the heart of the earth.
Black men are the tall trees that remain
Standing in a forest after a fire.

Williams, 1995, p. 71

In the metaphors of this poem, *Black Man* is the strong and forbidding structure which guards and protects his counterpart, offspring, and environment from potential destruction. *Black Woman*, Mother Earth, not only thrives under the support of the trees but serves as the foundation from which tall trees stretch, bloom, and flourish. *Mother Earth* is the bearer and nurturer from which the forest with its tall trees gathers sustenance, strength, and endurance. Without Earth there would be no forest; there would be no trees; there would be no life. Without the forest of trees, whose roots stretch deep into the Earth, Nature's elements would strip the life-force from Earth.

Nature teaches universal balance of female and male energies and is the foundation for survival and regeneration of the species, the family, and the ecology. When vision is obscured to reveal only individual or small groups of trees; the entire forest is veiled, over-shadowed, and illusory. Interlocking relationships remain a mystery. Clarifying the vision of trees, forest, fire, and the interdependent earth aids in lifting the potentially treacherous and deleterious cloak of obscurity. We begin with a link between specific elements, gender, and coupling. The elements, as the Fali people of Africa teach us, bind humans to the universe and are divided into two couples: Fire (male) and Earth (female), and Air (male) and Water (female). Diverse elements are bound to each other in an interdependent and meaningful relationship: Seeds are bound to fire, fish to water, mammals to the earth, and birds to the air (Erny, 1973; Knappert, 1990).

African perspectives of these elements emphasize the link with the spiritual or Divine force which flows through all beings and things. "What ever is, is in the first place spirit." Spirit is the African reality as it permeates everything that is. To be, is to be spirit since everything in the cosmos is connected through spirit. Elements, from an African and spirit perspective, serve as a foundation for the male-female balance that is found in nature.

Balance in Manhood and Womanhood Socialization

Emotional and psychological trust and unconditional love between adult men and women serve not only the security of the couple–they are the basis for trust in family and community. The story of Isis and Osiris explains this critical bond.

> We understand why Isis labored so diligently to reclaim the scattered pieces of Osiris's body: Isis knew she existed because Osiris existed; Osiris knew he existed because Isis existed. Their individual existence would not have been possible, would not have had meaning without the existence of the other. For males and females have multifaceted relationships to one another. Isis is mother, sister and wife to malehood. Osiris is son, brother, husband, and father to femalehood. (Chinyelu, 1995, p. 11)

The essential man-woman pair creates balance and integral roles in all of our strategies for success. Equality and balance between men and women can be traced back to ancient Kemet (Egypt). It is found in the messages of our ancestors, in the stories of nature, and in the non-sexist spiritual principles of the twinned and complementary universe. These concepts serve as a foundation and guide our recovery and reafrikanization in male and female socialization.

Traditional African Socialization for Manhood and Womanhood

Among Africans it is believed that the new child is different from adults because they are not fully developed (analogous to the unripe grain which cannot reproduce), androgynous and bisexual carrying at the same time the male and female principle. According to Erny (1973) newborn infants inherit both the soul and the double of a deceased person. At the time of delivery the two join with the baby, in reversed roles. The double is merged with the body of the child and makes up the soul. The soul of the dead person merges with delivery waters spread on the ground and makes up the shadow, which becomes the double, or twin. A baby boy has a female double and a baby girl's double will be male. This explanation of "the principle of duality, realized in the universe in the sky-earth opposition, is reflected in the person through the separation of sexes necessary for multiplication of the species" (Erny, 1973, p. 67). The adult, on the other hand, is distinctly determined by gender, being one or the other, but not both at the same time (Erny, 1973). The dual energies are cultivated to work within the roles needed for each to carry out their social, familial, and community responsibilities.

These principles of African cosmology and gender complementarity reviewed in the preceding sections are the foundation for the socialization of males and females. Transformation or the transition from child to adult for the African requires three major components, without which the person can never arrive at adult status. Spirit, communal self-knowledge—which includes the people's sacred history, and gender roles are the three essential components of the African person and therefore serve as the traditional context for bringing the boy to manhood and the girl to womanhood. Eliade (1958) provides a clear analysis and explanation of the interconnectedness of these three elements (spirit, self-knowledge, gender) of adulthood in traditional societies. The longing for rebirth is a human instinct and the seed of creation for the many initiatory customs of all peoples. First, a people's sacred history originates with the explanation of how the world and humans came to be. This is the basis for human behavior and all social and cultural institutions. In all creation stories, humans are created and socialized by a supernatural being or forces. Novices gain access to traditional knowledge or sacred history by way of ordeals, secret ceremonies, and extended teachings from elders/initiators. The main contributor to this requirement for adult status is the puberty rite or adolescent passage to adulthood.

All African societies have what have come to be known as rites of passage marking the movement of age set groups from one stage of spirit/life to another (see Moore et al., 1987; Mbiti, 1991; Opoko, 1977; Warfield-Coppock, 1990; 1992; 1994). Once a child transfers from the community of the spirits and is welcomed into its physical family and community, he or she journeys through life stages which eventually cycle back to the spirit community (at death). The very young and very old are closest to the spiritual world and are therefore known to have strong access to the lessons from the other side. Short of training or preparation, this is the way that humans are naturally in touch with those (ancestors) in the realm of the invisible (Diallo & Hall, 1989). The family and community are responsible for guiding all persons through their journey on earth (in the physical world). The essence of one's spirit remains visible to those willing and capable of abiding in the African reality.

The traditional training of the boy and girl to adulthood has its similarities and its differences. The five components of traditional rite of passage for males and females are: (1) preparation of the sacred ground, (2) separation from the mother, (3) symbol of initiatory death, (4) initiatory ordeals and, (5) initiatory rebirth/collective regeneration (Warfield-Coppock & Coppock, 1992). These common themes will be presented first followed by a review of some of the differences between the male and female rites.

Preparation of the Sacred Ground. During the preparation stage adults (initiators) come together to make arrangements and provisions for the initiates and the sacred ground. The arrangements may include erecting enclosures, constructing sacred emblems or symbols, a ritual cleansing, libation or communications with the spiritual world, marking off paths and a circular ring of ground upon which the ceremonies will take place. Separately, mature women and men prepare for the community's daughters and sons.

The symbol of the sacred ground is, first, the image of the world and, second, the world consecrated by the presence of the Supreme Being. The presence of the sacred ground embodies a reintegration of sacred Time when God or the ancestors began initiation for humans. Every initiation process and ceremony, then, is reliving the Time and Place of the original, Divine presence. It is at this time that the initiates are given the sacred history and the teachings of its symbols and traditions (Eliade, 1958).

Separation from Mother. Removing the child from its familiar surrounding and mother is the first step toward manhood or womanhood. The meaning is more dramatic for males which may be the reason that universally the male rites are more common and sensational than female practices. The children now remain in the company of the same gender adults or elders. For girls this may include their mothers, aunts, grandmothers. The rite of separation to an unknown situation is also a symbol of death. Some traditional societies do not socialize their girls in groups but send them to live with their grandmothers outside of the city environment for a period of time to learn the lessons of womanhood (personal communication, Marly, 1994).

Initiatory Death. The symbolism of initiatory death is a major component of traditional mythology. Upon separation, mothers are led to believe that their sons will die and mothers mourn as they would for the dead. Initiates are likewise fearful, as they are led to believe that they will be captured and killed. Until now, children have not participated in the religious life of their community and are generally unaware of what caused the death of those they have seen funeralized.

The symbol of death particularly for the male initiation relies on the need for a strong break from the mother. Mothers understand that when their sons are returned they will never again be their babies, but will be reborn as men. The boys will experience a darkness/unknown unlike any natural darkness they have known to date, symbolizing movement from darkness to light or from the profane maternal world to the sacred. The passage requires a death of one life to gain access to the other (Eliade, 1958). Many groups believe that the initiate is killed and resuscitated during the initiation process. Some people scar the skin or remove a tooth as a symbol of that connection with death. The Divinity who restores life also confers sexuality and fertility.

Initiatory Ordeals. The ordeals or challenges fall into three areas—physical, spiritual, and mental. Physical ordeals may include conquering physical fatigue (existing on little sleep or rest, going to bed late, rising early or during the night); dietary restrictions or fasting; restrictions against touching food or feeding self (symbolizing the baby-like state); restrictions against speech symbolizing infant state or death; silence of initiates is a common practice reinforcing their humility in the presence of adults and elders.

All of the physical ordeals or prohibitions, i.e., fasting, silence, darkness, suppression or restriction of sight to the ground, have corollary spiritual and/or mental interpretations. The initiate's preparation for adult life includes awakening to adult spiritual and mental life through concentration, problem-solving, bonding, and accessing the spiritual world through meditation/prayer, drumming, dancing and singing. The initiate is taught the people's sacred history and traditions as they are brought out of the darkness into the light (a spiritual knowledge). This custom of climbing a tree symbolizes ascension. The tree represents the axis of the cosmos with the novice desiring to reach divine or spiritual knowledge (Eliade, 1958).

Initiatory Rebirth and Collective Regeneration. The conclusion of the rite of passage is resuscitation or the symbolic awakening into the community of initiated men (or women). Girls and boys are regenerated from their profane condition of childhood, ignorance, and asexuality. Initiatory death and resurrection changes the initiate's fundamental mode of being, while revealing to him or her the sacredness of human life and of the world. The process begins the journey into adulthood with the revelation of the mysteries common to most religions–the interconnectedness of humans, the cosmos with all forms of life, God and deities (Eliade, 1958). The spirit of the initiated person is reborn. Physically the initiates receive new clothes, duties, responsibilities, and privileges as the community, in celebration (music, dance, feasting), welcomes them back.

Traditional Manhood Socialization

The masculine principle is largely associated with the archetype of Warrior or Protector. The male is secondarily father. However, to reach this ideal one must separate from the primary nurturer/mother. Symbolically and literally, the boy who is not taken to the forest by his father will remain forever his mother's baby. The physical, spiritual, and mental ordeals or challenges provided by mature warrior/protectors to the male child will ensure his break from the mothers' community and guarantee him a place among the community of men.

Circumcision is a physical ordeal largely associated with traditional practices. The first deity to perform circumcision was Atum-Ra on himself for the purpose of sacrifice of the female part of the male. This ritual was for the liberation of the man from the feminine/mother archetype permanently establishing him as exclusively masculine. Throughout Africa the uncircumcised male is considered a boy, unable to participate in the activities of men. When he is circumcised, at age 12-14 years with other members of his age set, he becomes responsible for the protection of his community. He is tested for courage, reliability, productivity, and skill until the age of 30 when, if successful, he is allowed to marry and later join the council of elders (Finch, 1991).

According to Erny (1973) the person in his or her natural state is equated with the condition of the uncircumcised child who is ignorant of his or her spirit. The ignorance and foulness, called *wanzo* among the Bambara, hinders knowledge, like a veil, of the self and

God. "All human training can be considered a fight against the wanzo. Circumcision contributes because it promotes enlightenment of the spirit by refining understanding" (pp. 69-70). Among the Dogon circumcision represents the cutting away of the female organ and loss of the greater part of femininity resulting in disequilibrium. In addition, the male initiate loses his androgynous harmony, marking the end of him as an individual. Consequently, he begins seeking what he lacks–the twinned unity in the union of husband and wife (Erny, 1973). During their rites initiates are given full knowledge of sex and marriage. They are taught to look forward to marriage as a duty to themselves, their parents and the clan (Kenyatta, 1965). A Maasai warrior and father taught his son that his rites which included circumcision means that he would be expected to give and not just receive, to protect the family and that no family affairs would be discussed without his consultation (Saitoti, 1986).

During training a Bassa initiate learns his responsibility is to "keep the flame alive in my father's house." He hears these words many times in the three months he spends in the forest learning to make himself ready to enter adult society. At the end of this difficult stage, and as though they had never heard the injunction before, the elders instruct their charges,

> Go now, and even if there seems to be no one in the entire compound, keep a flame burning in your father's house. The initiate then asks "who is father and what is Europe's impact on Africa?" "Confronted with the winds of change, the fire has dimmed and is dying in the house of the fathers"; "what must one do with the confused (especially by the ways of the West) youth of today and the loss of the Africans' traditional ways?" The answer given initiates by their elders is: Fire has no better friend than the wind. Wind can only destroy fire if it is covered or over-protected. Expose the fire to the winds, which will fan and blow it for you. As before the instruction is to add wood, remove the ashes and open it up. Today the world is father's compound. Tomorrow the universe will be father's compound, and our planet father's house. Move with the times. . . . A people is beaten in battle only when the sons fail

to re-build the shrines which have been destroyed. (Bassomb, 1995, p. 9-11)

It is essential that initiates learn these lessons of nature and the elements. The lessons of our ancestors and elders insist, even with changing time, that we pass on the ways, the knowledge, the shrines, the religions, the rites, training, and traditions of African people (see Mandela, 1994; Some, 1993, 1994). The work of understanding and socializing our young African-American males has become prominent in the research and community action. Writers are sharing their experiences of being guided into manhood or their observation of providing growth experiences for young males. Numerous rites practices for African-American sons have been created and documented in these publications (Chinyelu, 1995; Connor, 1995; Dunier, 1992; Gilmore, 1990; Hare & Hare, 1990; Hill, 1992; Johnson, 1995; Majors & Gordon, 1994; Perkins, 1992).

Traditional Womanhood Socialization

The feminine principle translates to the Mother archetype. Like the male, to reach this ideal one must separate from the androgynous and masculine principle. The girl, however, does not have to be ripped from her mother to become a woman. Still, there are physical, spiritual, and mental challenges provided by mature women to guide the girl to her place in the community of women. To begin, the girl must understand her people's sacred history and her essential role in it (Warfield-Coppock, 1994).

Woman, according to Finch (1991), is associated with the "four blood mysteries." Woman's mystical qualities included her changing body, the periodic menses, its cessation and flow again with her ability to bear and nurture new life. Menarche then became a time of celebration. In addition, the female was human's first time-keeper. The moon, originally feminine, was identified with its changing phases over a 291/2 day period and became a celestial calendar linked to the menstrual cycle because of their seeming coincidence. The woman, on account of her natural periodicity, is, as Newmann (1955) calls her, "a type of time," for she was the first guardian of time. It was not until later, when patriarchal rule emerged and took hold, that strict taboos surrounded females and the flow of menstrual blood became the "curse."

Researchers acknowledge the primacy of the feminine principle within the spiritual realm (Boone, 1986; Finch, 1991; Jefferies, 1984; Sarpong, 1977; T'Shaka, 1995; Turner, 1987; Yarbrough, 1984), in addition to the prominent role of religion or spirituality in the lives of Africans (Hackett, 1991; Niangoran-Bouah, 1991; Olupona, 1991; Opoku, 1977; Some, 1993, 1994). Among traditional African societies women, due to their mystical qualities were foremost in maintaining the connection with the unseen and the health of the people.

> It was believed that the mixture of the correct elements could be used to inspire and maintain the favorable disposition of the seen and the unseen forces (the gods) that surround and work within the individual and the community. If a ceremonial dance had all the correct component parts; the correct entreaty to the Gods for favorable intercession, the correct dance movements, rhythms, dress, attitude, correct closing and purpose, then that dance was considered to be life-giving and therefore good and beautiful. *Beauty is as beauty does.* (Yarbrough, 1984, p. 89)

The primacy of the feminine is found in many spiritual works. Additionally, a high regard and value for women is noted in traditional African societies (Mbiti, 1991; Omoyajowo, 1991; Van Sertima, 1984; Woodman, 1989). Sarpong (1977) shares the importance of women and the balance provided in the societies of the Ashanti kingdom. He discusses: (1) the girl during the nubility rites; (2) the queen-mother and; (3) the role of the sister. Sacredness of girls is said to be symbolized by the stool. Songs are chanted while the girls are carried to the riverside for the ritual bath (at this time she is called "queen-mother").

According to Richards (1982), among women there is a generalized authority of older women which cuts across authority, based on lines of descent: "The mother's role in rearing her daughter to physical maturity ends when she 'gives her daughter to the nacimbusa' who tests the girl's fitness for motherhood and admits her to the community of married women" (Richards, 1982, p. xxv). The *nacimbusa* (midwife) is expected to deliver the first child of each girl she initiates, remain her advisor throughout her married life, and instruct her in all practical (care of spouse and children) and women's matters.

Daughters of African-Americans are now being provided with similar relationships teaching women's and motherhood roles (Collins, 1991; Moore et al., 1987; Warfield-Coppock, 1994). Hundreds of programs have evolved in the last decade. Documentation of the girl's rite of passage process in *Transformation: A Rites of Passage Manual for African American Girls*, was published in 1987 by four mothers (Moore, Gilyard, King-McCreary, & Warfield-Coppock) prompting churches, sororities, women's organizations, community groups, boys and girls clubs, to take responsibility for passing on African women's knowledge to both biological and nonbiological daughters.

The Challenge of Cultural Oppression and the Maafa to African Manhood and Womanhood Socialization

A significant challenge to contemporary manhood and womanhood socialization is the continuing impact of the Maafa (also known as the African Holocaust). Eurocentric or sub-optimal domination and the plethora of destructive strategies have all but obliterated the spiritual and cultural practices of African people. Despiritualization has resulted in maladaptive and self-destructive thought and behavioral practices. The effects of the Maafa on men and women, families, communities and their implications for man and womanhood development will be explored briefly.

> The smell of death was everywhere. It was in the woodland the tar of the ship's hull. It was in the creaky masts and the dingy canvas sails. The nasty hemp nets slashed to the sides of the ship to catch Africans who choose death in the Atlantic or Indian Oceans rather than remain enslaved. . . . the spirits of the dead moved among the living. So on those Death ships, spiritually sensitive Africans felt, saw, heard–experienced–the trapped Spirits of the Dead Ones. . . . Even when the slave ship was new, our ancestors felt the Death spirit and sang out a warning that needed no translation. (Anderson, 1995, p. 91)

The Maafa, defined as the source of psyche and spiritual destruction, is the continuous process of white supremacy and presence of racism (social, economic, political, religious, environmental, family, health) resulting in denying the validity of African people's humanity. The Maafa is the complete disregard and disrespect for Africa, her people's ancestry, and right to exist (Nobles, 1994b). As a result African people and their descendants have experienced systematic physical, mental, and spiritual destruction (Anderson, 1995; Bulhan, 1985; Cress-Welsing, 1991; Johnson & Leighton, 1995; Madhubuti, 1994; Perkins, 1986; Roberson, 1995; Wilson, 1993). This devastation, otherwise called the Maafian experience, is an ongoing consequence of European and white racism and domination.

A serious challenge to African culture and existence has been the forced adoption of Eurocentric cognitive style, values, behavior and its continuing genocidal effects. Researchers Wright (1980), Ani (1994), and Sowande (1973) have expounded on the European cultural pathology which has created the system of world domination and genocide defined as, "the deliberate and systematic destruction of a racial, political or cultural group by acts of omission and/or commission designed to destroy the life (spirit) force" (Nobles, 1994a, p. 6). The effects of genocide, oppression, and white supremacy on African men and women, its devastating consequences on the balance and harmony in relationships, in the family, community, and race has been discussed by many researchers and social scientists (Anderson, 1995; Ani, 1994; Welsing, 1991; Gibbs, 1988; Harrison, 1988; Mauer, 1994; Monroe & Goldman, 1988; Nobles, 1994a; Nobles, 1994b; Perkins, 1986; Roberson, 1995; Stewart, 1994; Wilson, 1991). Perhaps the most profound genocidal effect upon the survival of African people is the harmony between men and women. Clearly, if an oppressor can separate and encourage conflict between progenitors and persuade the adoption of alien values and customs, the endurance and perhaps, even the existence of the people is at best, tenuous (Madhubuti, 1994). T'Shaka (1995) suggests that alienation is created by adopting a world view of "the strong rule the weak" over the "equally empowered" governed male and female society:

The alienation of masculine from feminine has produced an alienation between male and female. This dual alienation leads to the "will-to-power" which worships the material and reduces the spiritual to the realm of superstition. Masculine-feminine, male-female alienation produces a despiritualization of humanity and an alienation between western humanity and the cosmos. . . . Progressively, the Western mind has torn itself away from its earlier African spiritual teachings, and embraced a materialistic, despiritualized world view devoid of truth and morality. (T'Shaka, 1995, p. 63)

A Contemporary Model for Male and Female Socialization

The state of contemporary male-female relationships exemplifies the destructive effects of alien culture on each group, culminating in a lack of balance, harmony, and reciprocity. Man-woman relationships must be rebuilt in the image of the loving, respectful units which served to fortify our people's will to survive and thrive. The model of reafricanization in Figure 1 depicts some common elements for African men and women. It melds the theory of reafrikanization with the activities and practices necessary to assist us in arriving at this long range goal of optimal living in an African reality. It suggests that the complementary nature of African socialization of man and womanhood training are essential components in the rediscovery process necessary for reafrikanization. While this model is visionary in scope it is not hypothetical. There are many groups, organizations, and communities developing and operating at various levels of the model. Four fundamental components of the model will be described in this section: (1) the reafrikanization process; (2) reinstitution of universal values; (3) personal within group transformations and; (4) group/society development. This author's experience with groups and communities across the U.S. will serve as examples.

The reafrikanization process is the basis for appropriate training for men and women of African descent which is inclusive of a

FIGURE 1. Model for Reafrikanization Using Group and Personal Transformation in Parallel Life Cycle Rites of Passage: Core Values, Manhood, Womanhood and Role Socialization

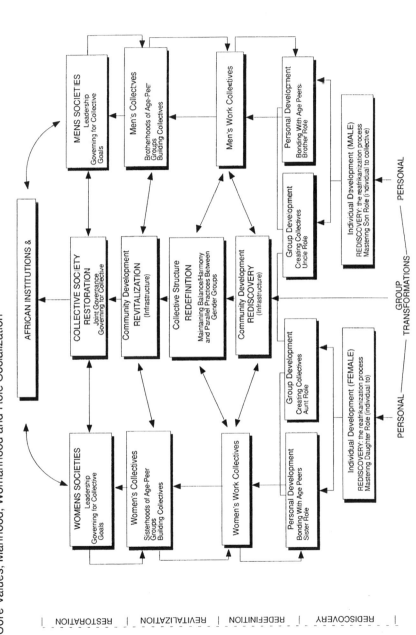

tri-level process articulated by Kwame Agyei Akoto (1992) in his text *Nation building*. Reafrikanization includes:

a. The *rediscovery* of core values of antiquity and surviving traditional societies, philosophy, language, and sacred works providing a consistent definition of African centered paradigm including appropriate behaviors and model of male-female balance. African religions are important to the rediscovery movement and the development of an African personal identity. African religions have a new/renewed home in communities in the U.S. Traditional religious practices and rituals can be seen in self-help books (Afua, 1992; Van Zant, 1992), in Black churches and organizations (Imani Temple, The Association of Black Psychologists). Core values appearing along the right side of the model urge mastery as one moves upward in the schematic.

b. *Redefinition* and cultural reaffirmation includes building Pan African institutional infrastructure and identifies appropriate defense, educational, and industrial development. At the same time people of African descent must use selective adaptation of nonAfrican technology while abandoning culturally-alienating behaviors, institutions, philosophy, religions, language, and methods. Nontraditional languages like Kiswahili, Yoruba, and Twi are offered at Black colleges such as Lincoln University.

c. *Revitalization* of liberating values, customs, and behaviors. Simultaneously, there is a stripping away of nonAfrican, maladaptive philosophy, customs and behaviors while building essential liberating, ascending and illuminating behaviors and philosophies. An example is our Black community's increasing observance of the African-American holiday Kwanzaa–a celebration of traditional African values.

d. *Restoration* calls for reestablishing, within our contemporary context, those principles, practices, and institutions which have ensured our survival to date. These include male-female balance and equality in leadership garnered from our study of African-based societies, recapturing essential elements of the African world view, philosophy, customs, and behaviors. These Africanisms have traditionally supported and enhanced the growth and development of all members of African descent communities (Holloway, 1990). T'Shaka (1995) reminds us that liberation for Africa and the diaspora depends upon accepting and strengthening the traditions of male-female equality. African men need not fear this vision as a threat to their manhood. For African women this just vision empowers her to draw from her strong creative masculine side, while nurturing her sensitive, intuitive, loving feminine side (Heiss, 1988; Obenga, 1992).

Afrikanization includes rites of passage, a collective journey through the life cycle, and a clear understanding of the completeness of the male roles (son, brother, uncle, husband, father, grandfather) and female roles (daughter, sister, aunt, wife, mother, grandmother) (Coppock, 1996). The process begins at the bottom of this model and incorporates progressively higher African principles/values and practice (respect, harmony, reciprocity, Maat[2], partnership, and equality) at each level before moving up to the next plateau. The female and male roles are mastered in the intricate relationships at each level of the collective. The roles move from daughter and son (showing respect and humility to parents and elders) to sister and brother (exhibiting care, love and support to age peers) to aunt and uncle (taking responsibility for other's children) to wife and mother and husband and father (maintaining a loving and nurturing environment and giving priority to one's children, spouse, and extended family) and finally to elder/grandmother and grandfather (sitting on advisory and governing councils; overseeing all affairs and passages in the community). Learning and practicing these roles provides for a return to traditional kinship practices which can be seen in strong and competent individuals, families, and organizations of African-Americans (Warfield-Coppock, 1985). An example is the national organization of rites of passage groups, the Afrikan National Rites of Passage United Kollective. ANROPUK encourages and offers educational forums for the development and stability of both male and female rites programs. Leadership is composed of male and female members with elders playing important advisory roles. Although members (groups and communities) have achieved varying levels of maturity they all practice African centered values, either Kemetic values or the Nguzo Saba (the seven principles used at Kwanzaa).

CONCLUSION

This treatise has sought to clarify the connection between manhood and womanhood training and the importance of placing this discourse in an African centered conceptual framework based on universal laws and the complementarity of opposites. This framework enhances our understanding of optimal systems of self-knowledge, positive cultural identity, and balanced interpersonal relationships. It counters the impact of the Maafa, which is the source of continuing oppression and despiritualization and maladaptive, self-destructive thought and behavioral practices. The adoption of alien values and cultural customs by African people has been destructive to man-woman relationships.

Reafrikanization is the antidote for the poison of the Maafa. The four stage map of rediscovery, redefinition, revitalization, and restoration can be used by any person, group, family, organization, and community to create an optimal conceptual system and life practices, positive cultural identity and balanced interpersonal relationships. Twinship and complementarity in nature and in humans is the backdrop for the traditional and current socialization practices (rites of passage across the life cycle) as well as the gender specific concepts and activities for males and females in contemporary African-American groups and communities.

Training for men and women can provide an appropriate African frame of reference—African centeredness, spirituality, knowledge of the sacred history, personal-within-group transformation, balance and harmony in male-female relationships, a return to equal partnership, reciprocity, and respect. Our ancestors remind us of this profound connection: "It is hard to fell a tree that is leaning against a rock."

NOTES

1. Universal laws are the principles thought to govern the relationships of Nature and humankind from the beginning of time. These ethics, spiritually based, direct and guide the action of the natural elements and the conduct of humans. It follows the concept that every event has purpose and meaning; nothing happens coincidentally.

2. Maat is a Kemetic (Egyptian) principle meaning righteousness, truth and justice. Derived from the practice of weighting the heart of a person before they travel to the other side at death. The heart must weigh no more than a feather (Maat's symbol) if one is deserving of a place in eternity.

REFERENCES

Afua, Q. (1992). *Heal thyself: For health and longevity.* Brooklyn: A & B Book Publishers.

Akoto, K. A. (1992). *Nation building: Theory and practice in African centered education.* Washington, DC: Pan Afrikan World Institute.

Amen, R.U.N. (1990a). *Metu Neter, Vol. 1: The great oracle of Tehuti and the Egyptian system of spiritual cultivation.* Bronx, NY: Khamit Corp.

Amen, R.U.N. (1990b). *Metu Neter, Vol. 2: Anuk Ausar: The Kamitic Initiation System.* Bronx, NY: Khamit Corp.

Anderson, S.E. (1995). *The Black holocaust for beginners.* New York: Writers and Readers Publishing.

Ani, M. (1994). *Yurugu: An African-centered critique of European cultural thought and behavior.* Trenton, NJ: African World Press.

Bassomb, N. (1995). IKOP MGOB: An account of an African child initiation. In H. Boyd & R.L. Allen (Eds.), *Brotherman: The odyssey of Black men in America,* pp. 9-11. New York: Ballentine.

Boone, S. A. (1986). *Radiance from the waters: Ideals of feminine beauty in Mende art.* New Haven: Yale University Press.

Bulhan, H.A. (1985). *Frantz Fanon and the psychology of oppression.* New York: Plenum Press.

Chinyelu, M. (1995). *Sons of the prophet: 9 inspirational stories about African men and boys in the land of captivity.* New York: Visions.

Collins, P. H. (1991). The meaning of motherhood in Black culture and Black mother-daughter relationships. In Bell-Scott, P. et al. (Eds.), *Double stitch: Black women write about mothers and daughters.* Boston, MA: Beacon.

Connor, M. K. (1995). *What is cool? Understanding Black manhood in America.* New York: Crown.

Coppock, B.A. (1996). *African American male afrikanization, socialization, and development: Recognizing and filling in developmental gaps.* Unpublished paper in progress.

Courlander, H. (1996). *The treasury of African folklore.* New York: Marlowe.

Cress-Welsing, F. (1991). *The Isis papers: The keys to the colors.* Chicago: Third World Press

Diallo, Y. & Hall, M. (1989). *The healing drum: African wisdom teachings.* Rochester, VT: Destiny Books.

Duneier, M. (1992). *Slim's table: Race, respectability, and masculinity.* Chicago, IL: The University of Chicago Press.

Eliade, M. (1958). *Rites and symbols of initiation: The mysteries of birth and rebirth.* New York: Harper and Row.

Erny, P. (1973). *Childhood and the cosmos: The social psychology of the Black African child.* New York: New Perspectives.

Evans, H. L., & Evans, R. C. (Summer, 1995). Coping stressors and depression among middle class African men. *Journal of African American Men, 1*(1), 29-40.

Finch, C.S. (1991). *Echoes of the old darkland: Themes from the African Eden.* Decatur, GA: Khenti, Inc.

Gibbs, J.T. (Ed.) (1988). *Young, Black, and male in America: An endangered species.* Dover, MA: Auburn House.

Gilmore, D.D. (1990). *Manhood in the making: Cultural concepts of masculinity.* New Haven: Yale University Press.

Hackett, R.I.J. (1991). Revitalization in African traditional religion. In J.K. Olupona (Ed.), *African traditional religions in contemporary society.* (pp. 135-148). New York: Paragon House.

Haich, E. (1974). *Initiation.* Palo Alto, CA: Seed Center.

Hare, N. & Hare, J. (1990). *Bringing the Black boy to manhood: The passage.* San Francisco, CA: Black Think Tank.

Harrison, A.O. (1988). Attitudes toward procreation among Black adults. In H.P. MacAdoo (Ed.), *Black families* (pp. 215-225). Newbury Park, CA: Sage.

Hawkins, B. (1996). The Black student athlete: The colonized Black body. *Journal of African American Men, 1*(3), 23-35.

Heiss, J. (1988). Women's values regarding marriage and the family. In H.P. MacAdoo (Ed.), *Black families* (pp. 201-214). Newbury Park, CA: Sage.

Hilliard, A. (1986). Pedagogy in ancient Kemet. In M. Karenga & J.H.Carruthers, (Eds.), *Kemet and the African worldview: Research, rescue, and restoration.* Los Angeles, CA: University of Sankore Press.

Hill, P. Jr. (1992). *Coming of age: African American rites-of-passage.* Chicago: African American Images.

Holloway, J.E. (1990). *Africanisms in American culture.* Bloomington, IN: Indiana University Press.

Jefferies, R. (April, 1984). The image of woman in African cave art. *The Journal of African Civilizations, 6*(1), 98-122. (Special issue Van Sertima, I. (Ed.) Black women in antiquity).

Johnson, W.E. (Spring, 1995). Paternal identity among urban adolescent males. In R. J. Taylor & J. Berry, (Eds.), *African American research perspectives: An occasional report 2*(1), 82-86. Ann Arbor, MI: Institute for Social Research.

Johnson, R., & Leighton, P.S. (1995). Black genocide? Thoughts on the plight of America's poor Black men. *Journal of African American Men, 1*(1), 3-21.

Kenyatta, J. (1965). *Facing Mount Kenya: The tribal life of the Gikuyu.* New York: Vintage.

King, R.D. (1990). *African origins of biological psychiatry.* Germantown, TN: Seymour-Smith.

King, L.M., Dixon, V.J., & Nobles, W.W. (Eds). (1976). *African philosophy: Assumptions and paradigms for research on Black persons.* Los Angeles, CA: Fanon Center Publication.

Knappert, J. (1990). *African mythology: An encyclopedia of myths and legends.* Hammersmith, England: Diamond Books.

MacAdoo, J.L. (1988). The roles of Black fathers in the socialization of Black children. In H.P. MacAdoo (Ed.), *Black families* (pp. 257-269). Newbury Park, CA: Sage.

Madhubuti, H. (1994). The west, Africa and the new millennium. In H. Madhubuti, *Claiming earth.* Chicago, IL: Third World Press.

Mandela, N.R. (1994). *Long walk to freedom: The autobiography of Nelson Mandela.* Boston, MA: Little, Brown.

Mauer, M. (1994). A generation behind bars: Black males and the criminal justice system. In R.G. Majors & J.U. Gordon (Eds.), *The American Black male: His present status and his future* (pp. 81-94). Chicago, IL: Nelson-Hall.

Mbiti, J.S. (1989). *African religions and philosophy, 2nd ed.* Great Britain: Heinemann International.

Mbiti, J.S. (1991). Flowers in the garden: The role of women in African religion. In J.K. Olupona (Ed.), *African traditional religions in contemporary society* (pp. 59 - 80). New York: Paragon House.

Mincy, R.B. (Ed.). (1994). *Nurturing young Black males: Challenges to agencies, programs, and social policy.* Washington, DC: The Urban Institute.

Mirza, H.S. (1992). *Young, female and Black.* London: Routledge.

Monroe, S. & Goldman, P. (1988). *Brothers: Black and poor–A true story of courage and survival.* New York: Ballentine.

Moore, M., Gilyard, G., King-McCreary, K. & Warfield-Coppock, N. (1987). *Transformation: A rites of passage manual for African American girls.* New York: STARS Press.

Myers, L.J. (1988). *Understanding an Afrocentric world view: Introduction to an optimal psychology.* Dubuque, IA: Kendall/Hunt.

Myers, L.J. (1991). Expanding the psychology of knowledge optimally: The importance of world view revisited. In R. Jones, *Black psychology, 3rd Ed.* (pp. 15-25). Berkeley, CA: Cobb & Henry.

Neumann, E. (1955). *The great mother: An analysis of the archetype.* Princeton, NJ: Princeton University Press.

Niangoran-Bouah, G. (1991). The talking drum: A traditional African instrument of liturgy and of meditation with the sacred. In J.K. Olupona (Ed.), *African traditional religions in contemporary society* (pp. 81-92). New York: Paragon House.

Nobles, W.W. (Oct., 1994a). Reclaiming Our Traditions. *Psych Discourse, 25*(10), 4-11.

Nobles, W.W. (1994b). *The African Maafa developmental plan and study guides.* San Francisco, CA: San Francisco State University.

Obenga, T. (1992). *Ancient Egypt and Black Africa: A student's handbook for the study of ancient Egypt in philosophy, linguistics & gender relations.* London, England: Karnak House.

Olupona, J.K. (Ed.). (1991). *African traditional religions in contemporary society.* New York: Paragon House.

Omoyajowo, J.A. (1991). The role of women in African traditional religion among the Yoruba. In J.K. Olupona (Ed.), *African traditional religions in contemporary society* (pp. 73-80). New York: Paragon House.

Opoku, K.A. (1977). *West African traditional religion.* Accra, Ghana: FEP.

Perkins, U.E. (1986). *Harvesting new generations: The positive development of Black youth.* Chicago, IL: Third World Press.

Perkins, U.E. (1992). *Afrocentric socialization paradigm for the positive development of Black males.* Chicago, IL: Assoc. for the Positive Development of Black Youth.

Polite, V. C. (1994). Reproduction and resistance: An analysis of African-American males response to schooling. In M.J. Shujaa (Ed.), *Too much schooling, too little education: A paradox of black life in white societies* (pp. 183-201). Trenton, NJ: African World Press.

Richards, A. (1988). *Chinsungu: A girl's initiation ceremony among the Bemba of Zambia.* London: Routledge.

Roberson, E.D. (1995). *The Maafa and beyond.* Columbia, MD: Kujichagulia.

Saitoti, T.O. (1986). *The worlds of a Maasai warrior: An autobiography.* Berkeley, CA: University of California Press.

Sarpong, P. (1977). *Girls' nubility rites in Ashanti.* Tema, Ghana: Ghana Publishing.

Serequeberhan, T. (1991). *African philosophy: The essential readings.* New York, NY: Paragon House.

Some, M.P. (1994). *Of water and spirit.* New York: G.P. Putnam's Sons.

Some, M.P. (1993). *Ritual: Power, healing and community.* Portland, OR: Swan/Raven.

Sowande, F. (1973). The quest of an African worldview: Utilization of African discourse. In J. Daniels (Ed.), *Black communications,* Project No. EH 6404-72-216. Washington, D.C.: The National Endowment for the Humanities.

Stewart, J.B. (1994). Neoconservative attacks on Black families and the Black male: An analysis and critique. In R.G. Majors & J.U. Gordon (Eds.), *The American Black male: His present status and his future* (pp. 39-58). Chicago, IL: Nelson-Hall.

T'Shaka, O. (1995). *Return to the African mother principle of male and female equality: Volume 1.* Oakland, CA: Pan Afrikan Publishers.

Turner, V. (1987). Betwixt and between: The liminal period in the rites of passage. In L. C. Mahdi, S. Foster & M. Little, *Betwixt and between: Patterns of masculine and feminine initiation.* LaSalle, IL: Open Court.

Van Sertima, I. (April, 1984). The African Eve: Introduction and summary. *The Journal of African Civilizations, 6*(1), 5-11.

Van Zant, I. (1992). *Tapping the power within: A path to self-empowerment for Black women.* New York: Harlem River Press.

Warfield-Coppock, N. (1985). *A qualitative study of the African American organization: Investigating Africanisms.* Doctoral dissertation completed at The Fielding Institute, Santa Barbara, CA. Ann Arbor, MI: University Microfilms, No. 88-24, 253.

Warfield-Coppock, N. (1990). *Afrocentric theory and applications, Volume 1: Adolescent rites of passage.* Washington, D.C.: Baobab Associates.

Warfield-Coppock, N. (Fall, 1992). The rites of passage movement: A resurgence of African-centered practices for socializing African American youth. *The Journal of Negro Education, 61* (4), 471-482.

Warfield-Coppock, N. (1994a). The rites of passage: Extending education into the African-American community. In M.J. Shujaa (Ed.), *Too much schooling, too little education: A paradox of black life in white societies* (pp. 377-393). Trenton, NJ: African World Press.

Warfield-Coppock, N. & B.A. Coppock (1992). *Afrocentric theory and applications, Volume 2: Advances in the Adolescent rites of passage.* Washington, D.C.: Baobab Associates.

Warfield-Coppock, N. (1994b). *Images of African sisterhood: Initiation and rites of passage to womanhood.* Washington, DC: Baobab Associates.

Williams, E.A. (Fall, 1995). Keep the candle burning: Morehouse College into the 21st century. *Journal of African American Men, 1*(2), 71-86.

Wilson, A.N. (1991). *Understanding Black adolescent male violence: Its remediation and prevention.* New York: Afrikan World InfoSystems.

Wilson, A.N. (1993). *The falsification of Afrikan consciousness: Eurocentric history, psychiatry and the politics of white supremacy.* New York: Afrikan World InfoSystems.

Woodman, M. (1987). From concrete to consciousness: The emergence of the feminine. In L. C. Mahdi, S. Foster & M. Little (Eds.), *Betwixt and between: Patterns of masculine and feminine initiation.* LaSalle, IL: Open Court.

Wright, B. (1984). *The psychopathic racial personality.* Chicago: Third World Press.

Yarbrough, C. (April, 1984). Female style and beauty in ancient Africa: A photo essay. *The Journal of African Civilizations, 6* (1), 86-97.

Prospects and Challenges
for African-American Manhood

Robert J. Jagers

University of Illinois at Chicago

Roderick J. Watts

DePaul University

There can be little debate over the need to enhance the life chances of African-Americans, especially those living in poor urban communities. To date, the vast human potential residing within this segment of society remains largely unrealized. It has been customary for observers to offer either a system-blame or a person-blame explanation for these circumstances. Instead, we find it useful to conceive of the "arrested development" of African-Americans as being rooted in and perpetuated by a complex constellation of internal and external psychological and structural barriers. Thus, although it is clear that cultural racism (Jones, 1989) continues to shape the opportunity structure for African-Americans, it is also apparent that some of their own thoughts and behaviors hamper movement toward well-being and liberation.

African-American men, especially these from low-income backgrounds, occupy a unique position in this scenario. European American hegemony and practice has convinced many African-American

---

[Haworth co-indexing entry note]: "Prospects and Challenges for African-American Manhood." Jagers, Robert J., and Roderick J. Watts. Co-published simultaneously in *Journal of Prevention & Intervention in the Community* (The Haworth Press, Inc.) Vol. 16, No. 1/2, 1997, pp. 147-155; and: *Manhood Development in Urban African-American Communities* (ed: Roderick J. Watts, and Robert J. Jagers) The Haworth Press, Inc., 1997, pp. 147-155. Single or multiple copies of this article are available for a fee from The Haworth Document Delivery Service [1-800-342-9678, 9:00 a.m. - 5:00 p.m. (EST). E-mail address: getinfo@haworth.com].

147

boys and men that physical prowess should be emphasized to the neglect of other talents. While physical power gains men a measure of social status worldwide, this tendency has played into stereotypic images of African-American manhood, effectively narrowing the aspirations of young men. Ironically, it has also lead to African-American men being both revered and reviled. For example, tremendous financial rewards and cult-like adulation are enjoyed by a small group of high-profile athletes and entertainers. This has propelled legions of young men and boys to be preoccupied during their formative years with careers in the entertainment industry. Alternatively, a subset of young men have adopted, to varying degrees, a reactive criminal lifestyle which was spawned by the market for illicit drugs. Drug trafficking and related activities have diminished the quality of life within the African-American community and have provided justification for the negative views of non-residents. The majority of boys and men are left in the lurch, possessing relatively little entertainment value, and having no criminal inclinations or background. Myopic views of African-American manhood force them to constantly and consistently reaffirm their humanity to themselves and others, while laboring to carry out their various social roles.

This volume was intended to aid in the construction of more holistic and progressive notions of African-American manhood. Most of the work contained herein proceeded from a psychological perspective–exploring issues of culture and race as they impact on the cognitive, emotional and behavioral characteristics of African-American boys and men. It was implied that pathways to desirable outcomes for African-American men must be informed by cultural and racial considerations. Indeed, there appeared to be a desire to articulate a set of core cultural beliefs and practices which could accommodate the existing diversity of African-American life, while also maximizing the prospects for long-term collective well-being.

In the following pages, we attempt to weave together some of the concepts and findings in this volume, with an eye toward future basic and applied research. Although low-income young men tended to be the focus of this issue, in the present exercise we highlight some of the points where socioeconomic matters might be relevant. We employ a developmental contextualist perspective because it allows us to consider salient person-context transactions that African-Americans must negotiate. We recognize that neither the people, nor their environment are static entities. The developmental trajectory of each influences, and is influenced, by that of the others. Ultimately, this perspective requires a theory that can accommodate a multi-layered, multivariate set of transactions, between and within family, community, national and global contexts. Theories in community psychology positing nested contexts and ecological theory that incorporates concepts such as succession to describe the development of social environments are all consistent with this perspective (Brofenbrenner, 1979, Kingry-Westergaard & Kelly, 1990). However, mapping the complex connections between micro, meso, macro and global systems is well beyond the scope of this discussion and the disciplines represented in this volume. A truly holistic approach would require an Afrographic analysis by an interdisciplinary team of political scientists, sociologists, economists, educators and the like. However, the exploration that follows seeks to touch on, from a psychological perspective, some of the intra- and inter-personal factors deemed relevant to this much needed integrative analysis of African-American social life.

DEVELOPMENTAL IMPERATIVES AND PATHWAYS

Determining what constitutes a healthy well-functioning man, and the supportive mechanisms for achieving such development are crucial concerns for the African-American community. Several contributors pointed to issues of spirituality as being a central ingredient in manhood. And families emerged as essential agents in men's development. The work of Warfield-Coppock can be seen as laying some conceptual foundations for much of this volume. She considered gender role development within traditional African thought and practice. It was suggested that a spiritually-derived notion of complimentarity forms the basis for interconnectedness, commitment and reciprocity in dyads and families. Rites of passage rituals were advanced as community sanctioned devices for instilling and confirming desired understanding and conduct by children and youth. One shortcoming of this important analysis was its failure to consider the hierarchical relationships, based on gender and other social indicators, which can be found in African societies. Critical examination of this oft-neglected reality is essential for discerning the intersections of power, privilege, duty and obligation within traditional culture and among contemporary African-heritage people.

The cultivation of spiritual well-being was the central interest in the preliminary study conducted by Mattis. Spiritual well-being connotes satisfaction both with one's relationship with God and with social others. College men and women did not differ in terms of their sense of spiritual well-being. Nor were there gender differences in endorsement of a spiritual orientation and external religious motivation, both of which emerged as positive predictors of spiritual well-being. Other gender differences did emerge which may warrant further attention. For example, men were found to have attended church less frequently while growing up, and to report religion to be less relevant to their self development currently. Further, men were less inclined than women to both indicate a need for faith and to attribute causality to God. The ability to generalize from these findings was limited by the use of retrospective data and by sample size and selectivity. However, this study provides a springboard for delving into the connection between spiritual and religious development, patterns of men's stress and coping, and subjective well-being.

Jagers submitted that a spiritual orientation conjoined with affective and communal orientations to form an Afrocultural social ethos. The connections between this ethos and good character were the basis for his integrity-based analysis of African-American social development. There were no gender or grade differences among third, sixth and seventh graders, and positive correspondence between children's ratings of themselves, their families and friends. Children's cultural phenomenology is important to desirable developmental outcomes. For example, the perception of a more Afrocultural family promoted greater "empathic concern" and more "social withdrawal" from peers engaging in negative behavior. Jagers saw these findings as evidence that families in risky community contexts promoted pro-social development in their youngsters. In addition, the perception of friends as more Afrocultural may buffer negative influences in the environment, minimize externalizing problem behavior and stimulate perspective-taking. A primary reliance on children's self-reports limited this research. There is a need for a more penetrating examination, from a developmental perspective, of the complex cultural reality of diverse populations and the implications for social functioning in various contexts.

The work of Stevenson converges with that of Jagers in important ways. In attempting to delineate adolescent boys' beliefs about parent's socialization messages, it was shown that a substantial portion of young men endorsed "proactive" or Afrocultural messages (e.g., emphasizing a spiritual orientation and communal family relations), while others identified "adaptive" (combining race awareness teaching with Afrocultural messages) or "protective" (race awareness) messages. Consistent with Jagers, the receipt of proactive messages corresponded with greater concern about potential physical harm, together with introversion and anger suppression. Interestingly, whether race awareness teaching occurred alone or with cultural grounding it positively associated with instrumental helplessness. Is this an unintended and adverse consequence of racial socialization? To answer that question, theorists need more specific information on the content and process of parental race awareness teaching. Stevenson's distinction between beliefs and experiences provides a point of departure for sampling more broadly the range, modes, agents and contexts of such communications. We construe this to be a task necessitating a mixed-method approach.

EMANCIPATORY INTERVENTION STRATEGIES

As Warfield-Coppock pointed out, the process of preparing young people for social roles is a critical cultural function. Families are cultural institutions where boys receive, through implicit and explicit means, the first inklings of what manhood is about. Ideally, their efforts are supported by other indigenous community institutions like peer groups, churches, schools and businesses. Cultural synchrony between these institutions can provide a narrow developmental pathway and, thereby, maximize outcomes for boys and young men. Findings of Jagers and Mattis provide glimpses of this possibility. However, as many families have disintegrated so too have many critical community institutions. They are often ineffective, experiencing a disjoint in their goals and practices and those of community residents–particularly young men and boys. Social and institutional disintegration has a profound effect on the life chances of all young people. Without these resources community-based support and control becomes less available. Requisite preparation and reinforcement for academic and social accomplishment don't occur and linkages to employment opportunities are nonexistent (Wilson, 1996). In turn, boys and young men become alienated from adults and disenchanted with prospects for conventional upward mobility. Substance abuse, academic underachievement, and interpersonal violence often accompany their seduction into the criminal economy.

In recent years there has been an explosion of primary and secondary interventions aimed at supplementing family efforts and reversing negative developmental trajectories for boys and men. Two programs described in this volume (Ghee, Walker & Younger ; Watts & Abdul-Adil) attempt to fill the socialization void through what can loosely be described as "manhood development" interventions. In many regards such programs prepare boys for more formal rites of passage programs. Acting as role models and mentors, the leaders of these and other similar manhood development programs attempt to provide some of the support, information and guidance traditionally provided by fathers and other male kith and kin. Unlike more conventional psycho-social programming that focuses exclusively on personal development, these programs have a cultural and sociopolitical emphasis informed by the unique historical circumstances of African-Americans. This can be discerned both in their curricular content and context.

In terms of content, both RAAMUS (Ghee, this volume) and Young Warriors (Watts, this volume) assume miseducation to be a core impediment to the personal and collective development of African-American boys. Thus there is an emphasis on helping participants to locate themselves in time and space. However, it appears that the programs diverge in terms of the age of their participants and in the central aims of their curricula. Ghee seeks to promote academic motivation and outcomes among pre- and early adolescents by addressing consonant (getting a good job, avoiding drugs) and competing (entertainment, peer acceptance) social concerns. Watts is more concerned with getting adolescent boys to develop critical thinking skills so that they can more effectively appraise themselves in the context of community disenfranchisement. The aim here was to facilitate a realization of one's participation in their own oppression and to subsequently promote dialogue around the conflation of personal and community change.

That neither of these programs addressed issues of spirituality was conspicuous in light of the centrality of this orientation in the work of the other contributors. In all, spirituality was implicated in integrity-based notions of manhood, subjective well-being, anger management, and pro-social attitudes. To the degree that such factors are important to the intervention processes and/or its outcomes, spirituality appears to be of some utility. Yet, how to effectively address such matters in school and community-based programs remains to be determined. It was also unclear how these programs treated issues of communalism. Communal relations can occur at the level of family, peers, race, or nation. While both programs sought to establish conceptual linkages with same race others, there was little evidence of efforts to develop practical interpersonal skills necessary to enhance relationships with family and friends. We wager that these more proximal relationships are more salient and that improvements in them will go a long way toward collective uplift. On the other hand, the Afrocultural orientations of orality, verve and rhythm/movement (Jagers, this volume) were central to the curricular context. These orientations become synergistic in the rap music employed by Watts. Both rap music and the multi-media strategy utilized by Ghee provide easy points of entry into the lives of the young men being served.

Data from both programs suggested that they have positive impacts on their participants. However, the utilization of within-subject designs limits our understanding of the impact of the programs. This is particularly true given the paucity of normative data on the cognitive, emotional and social development of African-American boys and men.

FUTURE RESEARCH AND ACTION

In the introduction to this volume we argued for the centrality of culture, gender, and liberation in theory and action in manhood development. The next step for action scholars is to create the relationships with community institutions necessary to move research and action beyond the small scale described in these articles. A systemic approach requires a systemic intervention, and none of the interventions described here consider the potential of their strategy for producing broad effects on community systems. Nor was much attention given to the long term viability of these strategies. Who will pay for them? What are the contradictions in funding progressive programs through government or foundation funds over the long term? In a word, *infrastructure* and organic, collaborative relationships with the communities of interest are needed to link these interventions with indigenous resources. Unfortunately, there is a catch-22 here. As noted previously, many of the problems these programs seek to reduce are due to oppression and severely limited indigenous resources. It may be fruitful to think about community development and social movements as the Black Panthers, the Nation of Islam, and M.L. King did, all of whom began their work in impoverished communities.

On the research side of the action-research coin, there is a need for basic research that further clarifies relationships between and among cultural transmission and acquisition, and intellectual and social attainment. It is an intuitively appealing one, but few investigators have examined it empirically. Critical treatments of traditional African thought and practice and derivative basic research are essential to pursue. The former is important because cultural socialization programs cannot succeed if they are not clear on the key cultural elements important to building healthy communities. Traditional practices are important to understand because they are steeped in the cultural sensibilities of interest, and they can help shape contemporary interventions. Similarly, the research on oppression and culturally-based urban pedagogy is quite limited. Efforts to develop new strategies for educating youth through research must inform future action efforts. Research and action are synergistic in manhood development. Communities and investigators both benefit from interventions with large numbers of participants and rigorous evaluation because movement toward liberation must be systematic and participatory. Both will benefit from the broad-based collaborations necessary to make programs function more like movements.

REFERENCES

Brofenbrenner, U. (1979). *The ecology of human development.* Cambridge: Harvard University Press.

Jones, J. (1989). Racism: A cultural analysis of the problem. in R. Jones (Ed.)., *Black Psychology* (3rd Ed.). Berkeley: Cobb & Henry.

Kingry-Westergaard, C., and Kelly, J. G. (1990). A contextualist epistemology for ecological research. In P. H. Tolan, C. Keys, F. Chertok, and L. Jason (Eds.), *Researching community psychology: The integration of theories and methods,* pp. 23-31. Washington D.C.: The American Psychological Association.

Wilson, W.J. (1996). *When work disappears.* NY: Knopf.

Index

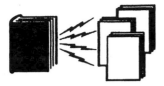

Haworth
DOCUMENT DELIVERY
SERVICE

This valuable service provides a single-article order form for any article from a Haworth journal.

- *Time Saving:* No running around from library to library to find a specific article.
- *Cost Effective:* All costs are kept down to a minimum.
- *Fast Delivery:* Choose from several options, including same-day FAX.
- *No Copyright Hassles:* You will be supplied by the original publisher.
- *Easy Payment:* Choose from several easy payment methods.

Open Accounts Welcome for . . .
- Library Interlibrary Loan Departments
- Library Network/Consortia Wishing to Provide Single-Article Services
- Indexing/Abstracting Services with Single Article Provision Services
- Document Provision Brokers and Freelance Information Service Providers

MAIL or *FAX* THIS ENTIRE ORDER FORM TO:

Haworth Document Delivery Service
The Haworth Press, Inc.
10 Alice Street
Binghamton, NY 13904-1580

or **FAX:** 1-800-895-0582
or **CALL:** 1-800-342-9678
9am-5pm EST

PLEASE SEND ME PHOTOCOPIES OF THE FOLLOWING SINGLE ARTICLES:

1) Journal Title: _____
    Vol/Issue/Year:_____Starting & Ending Pages:_____
Article Title:_____
_____

2) Journal Title: _____
    Vol/Issue/Year:_____Starting & Ending Pages:_____
Article Title:_____
_____

3) Journal Title: _____
    Vol/Issue/Year:_____Starting & Ending Pages:_____
Article Title:_____
_____

4) Journal Title: _____
    Vol/Issue/Year:_____Starting & Ending Pages:_____
Article Title:_____
_____

(See other side for Costs and Payment Information)

COSTS: Please figure your cost to order quality copies of an article.

1. Set-up charge per article: $8.00
   ($8.00 × number of separate articles) _____

2. Photocopying charge for each article:

   1-10 pages: $1.00 _____

   11-19 pages: $3.00 _____

   20-29 pages: $5.00 _____

   30+ pages: $2.00/10 pages _____

3. Flexicover (optional): $2.00/article _____

4. Postage & Handling: US: $1.00 for the first article/
   $.50 each additional article _____

   Federal Express: $25.00 _____

   Outside US: $2.00 for first article/
   $.50 each additional article _____

5. Same-day FAX service: $.35 per page _____

   GRAND TOTAL: _____

METHOD OF PAYMENT: (please check one)

❏ Check enclosed   ❏ Please ship and bill. PO # _____
(sorry we can ship and bill to bookstores only! All others must pre-pay)

❏ Charge to my credit card: ❏ Visa; ❏ MasterCard; ❏ Discover;
❏ American Express;

Account Number:_____ Expiration date:_____

Signature: *X*_____

Name: _____ Institution: _____

Address: _____

_____

City: _____ State:_____ Zip:_____

Phone Number: _____ FAX Number: _____

MAIL or *FAX* THIS ENTIRE ORDER FORM TO:

Haworth Document Delivery Service	**or FAX:** 1-800-895-0582
The Haworth Press, Inc.	**or CALL:** 1-800-342-9678
10 Alice Street	9am-5pm EST)
Binghamton, NY 13904-1580	